**Community Care
Practice Handbooks**

*General Editor:* **Martin Davies**

**Consultation**
An Aid to Successful Social Work

**Community Care
Practice Handbooks**

*General Editor:* Martin Davies

1 The Social Worker and The Courts – *David Wright*
2 Groupwork – *Allan Brown*
3 Intermediate Treatment and Social Work – *Ray Jones and Andrew Kerslake*
4 Social Work With Mentally Handicapped People – *Christopher Hanvey*
5 The Essential Social Worker: A Guide to Positive Practice – *Martin Davies*
6 Achieving Change in Social Work – *John and Mary Collins*
7 Alcohol Related Problems – *Linda Hunt*
8 Residential Care: A Community Resource – *Leonard Davis*
9 Working with the Elderly – *Eunice Mortimer*
10 Welfare Rights – *Ruth Cohen and Andrée Rushton*
11 Rights and Responsibilities – *Neil Leighton, Richard Stalley and David Watson*
12 Adolescents and Social Workers – *Margaret Crompton*
13 Children In and Out of Care – *Claire Wendelken*
14 Sex and the Social Worker – *Leonard Davis*
15 Consultation: An Aid to Successful Social Work – *Allan Brown*
16 Social Work and Health Care – *Andrée Rushton and Penny Davies*

# Consultation
## An Aid to Successful Social Work

Allan Brown

HEINEMANN EDUCATIONAL BOOKS
LONDON · EXETER (NEW HAMPSHIRE)

Heinemann Educational Books Ltd
22 Bedford Square, London WC1B 3HH
Heinemann Educational Books Inc
4 Front Street, Exeter, New Hampshire 03833
LONDON EDINBURGH MELBOURNE AUCKLAND
HONG KONG SINGAPORE KUALA LUMPUR NEW DELHI
IBADAN NAIROBI JOHANNESBURG
EXETER (NH) KINGSTON PORT OF SPAIN

© Allan Brown 1984
First published 1984

**British Library Cataloguing in Publication Data**

Brown, Allan
    Consultation.—(Community care
    practice handbooks; 15)
    1. Special service – Great Britain
    2. Medical consultation – Great Britain
    3. Psychiatric consultation – Great Britain
    I. Title    II. Series
    361.3'23'0941    HV41

    ISBN 0-435-82092-3

Typeset by the Castlefield Press, Moulton, Northampton
and printed by Biddles Ltd, Guildford, Surrey

For Celia

# Contents

*Acknowlegements* viii

*Introduction* ix

1 **Consultancy and Supervision** 1
definitions and distinctions; needs, sources and types of consultancy and supervision

2 **The Consultee** 18
needs and career-stages; learning and work-styles; preparation and contract; consultee skills; games in supervision

3 **The Consultant** 39
contact, contract and preparation; consultant skills, techniques and pitfalls; different types of consultancy and supervision

4 **The Student Stage** 56
preparation for placement, and self-management in the student-supervisee role; 'visible' practice and its supervision; theory, assessment

5 **Group Consultancy** 74
consultancy in groups, and group supervision; staff group consultancy

6 **Professional Development and the Team Context** 91

*Bibliography* 97

*Index* 100

# Acknowledgements

I am indebted to the many consultees and consultants, supervisors and supervisees, with whom I have worked over the years, and from whom I have learned so much. Whatever understanding I have managed to convey in this book owes much to their contribution to my own development.

My heartfelt thanks go to three colleagues each of whom not only read an entire draft of the book, making numerous invaluable comments and suggestions, but who also found time to discuss some of the content with me. They are: Peter Hawkins, freelance consultant and groupworker; Annette Holman, lecturer in social work at Bristol University; and John Hughes, Senior Probation Officer in Avon.

I was able to find time to write during a period of study-leave made possible by my colleagues in the Department of Social Work at Bristol University.

I am especially grateful to Yvonne Odjidja for undertaking all the typing and for patiently deciphering my handwriting.

My great good fortune is to have a full-time tandem consultant, my wife Celia, with whom the roles of consultant and consultee are exchanged very frequently to our mutual benefit.

# Introduction

The social worker's job is complex and demanding. It is often stressful. The first priority is to survive. After that, the aim is to be as effective as possible in responding to the needs of the people who come, or are sent or referred, to the agency. This requires a personal pool of skill, knowledge and experience which is constantly being widened and deepened in a process of renewal and development throughout the social worker's career. The essential contribution of consultancy and supervision* in ensuring both the survival and the improved quality of practice of social workers and other staff, and therefore the quality of service to clients, cannot be overestimated. I hope that this book may be of some value to those who are engaged in this process in their roles as both 'givers' and 'receivers'.

The approach taken in the book rests on several assumptions and attitudes which should be shared with the reader at the outset:

(1) Whilst the available evidence about standards of consultancy and supervision, and worker satisfaction/dissatisfaction with it, is mixed and not markedly unfavourable overall (see Stevenson and Parsloe 1978; Kadushin 1974; Hughes 1980; Satyamurti 1981) there is concern about variable provision and standards, and all would agree that there is room for improvement and adaptation to changing circumstances. In the UK in the early and mid 1970s, social work was characterised by rapid expansion, untrained inexperienced practitioners (at least in Social Services Departments) and rapidly promoted middle and senior managers. By contrast, in the early 1980s (and into the foreseeable future) we have a period of non-expansion and low mobility resulting in an increasing proportion of social work staff who are professionally trained, experienced, and often highly skilled. Their team leaders have often been middle-managers much longer than they were previously practitioners. Thus whilst the need for a strong supervisory element remains for students, unqualified workers (now mostly in residential work and day-care) and inexperienced qualified workers, there is a large and growing number of experienced competent practitioners who are extending the frontiers of skill and creative practice, who have both a need for skilled consultancy

---

* These terms are defined and discussed in Chapter 1, and some readers may find it useful to turn to the relevant section at this point.

(which their supervisor may or may not be able to offer) and a capacity to offer it to others. Adjustments are needed to meet these changing needs and resources.

(2) The perspective, needs and skills of the consultee and supervisee are generally neglected in the literature, which tends to assume a managerial perspective and focus on the role of the supervisor. This neglect is partly due to the pervasiveness of the bureaucratic model, but even those sources (e.g. Pettes 1979; Westheimer 1977) which emphasise a professional model tend to assume a rather hierarchical or paternalistic stance of 'expert helping novice', concentrating on the skills of the consultant or supervisor. To redress the balance, and because I am committed to an interactional approach, I shall be suggesting that the practitioner (however inexperienced, and starting at the student stage) be proactive in his approach to his own professional development and self-learning. There is as much to learn about the role and skills of being a supervisee/consultee/trainee as there is about a supervisor/consultant/trainer.

If a worker takes responsibility himself* for his own professional development, this is likely to be both more satisfying, and more productive for his work with clients, than if he is dependent on supervisors. He will of course need the resources, skills and facilitation of others to help him and he will need to be active in seeking this assistance. He will also need to recognise that as an agency employee he is not autonomous, and that periodically his work will be subject to checks by others. There is a close parallel here with some social work intervention models, for example task-centred casework (Reid and Epstein 1977) and social skills and personal problem-solving (Priestley *et al.* 1978), which encourage clients, as far as they are able and within the constraints set by legislative requirements, to take charge of their own problems and be active in seeking the help and resources they need.

(3) The 'novice' social worker often disbelieves that he has anything worthwhile to contribute to more experienced workers, and similarly there is sometimes an assumption that the very experienced practitioner (or manager) no longer needs help with his work. My assumption, based on experience, observation and a humanistic philosophy, is that every social worker, however experienced, needs consultancy help, and that every student or 'beginner',

---

* In this text the male gender will be used for those in the consultee *or* supervisee role, and the female gender for consultants and supervisors.

however inexperienced in social work, can contribute usefully to the consultancy needs of others. The type of need and what the person has to offer vary greatly, of course, according to the level of experience, but the principle remains that, right from the beginning of his career, the individual can, if he is allowed, be both helper and helped in his relationship with professional colleagues. The one-to-one role-relationship with a senior often obscures what the help-seeker might contribute, and this is more often revealed in group supervision, team-meetings and informal contexts, offering as they do, more opportunity for reciprocity

(4) The first experience of supervision whether as a student during training, or as an unqualified worker, is very important both as the first stage of a career-long process of professional development, and as a role-model often influencing future expectations and approaches quite disproportionately. One of the reasons why student supervision is included in this text is because the attitudes and roles taken by both the student and the practice-teacher or student-supervisor (yes, both titles are used, and convey rather different messages!) can be very influential in subsequent supervision and consultancy as a qualified worker. The structure of social work training, and indeed of our entire educational system, has too frequently in the past led to students approaching a placement in a passive reactive frame of mind. The model to be developed here has the opposite emphasis. It is one which emphasises the student's capacity to influence his own learning, and the practice teacher's skills in facilitating this process in her dual role of teacher and assessor.

(5) The individual's needs and resources must be set in the context of the social work team or staff-group (and behind that the agency) to which he belongs. There are some indications of a gradual shift from individualistic team models toward a more collective approach (these terms are used by Parsloe, 1981) in which resources are pooled, tasks shared and joint work occurs. An important part of this sharing is the identification and harmonisation of supervision and consultancy needs and resources at both individual and group levels. Professional and managerial functions meet uniquely in the pivotal role of the team-leader, and the team is the key location for the professional development of its members. This does not mean that it will always be the *source* of consultancy, professional development, training, or even supervision, but it is the place where the collective and individual needs and resources of its members can

be identified and decisions taken about how best to meet the needs and make use of the resources.

(6) In recent years increasingly diversified and imaginative approaches to consultancy have been developed. The traditional one-to-one session based on discussion is probably still the norm, but the range of possibilities now includes group and peer models, 'live' supervision, video and audio tapes, sculpting, role-play and so on. These techniques can enrich the possibilities and effectiveness of consultancy.

(7) No discussion of consultancy and supervision can ignore the profound influence of the organisational context of statutory social work and the bureaucratic-professional tensions inherent in pyramidical structures. Conflict is often masked (although actually it is highlighted) by the coincidence of the role of supervisor and consultant when the line-manager offers consultancy within the supervisory relationship. There has been much debate about the compatibility of uninhibited consultancy and managerial responsibility, and the extent to which the latter constrains the former. One drastic solution proposed by some is the 'dual model' (Munson 1979) in which administrative supervision offered by a supervisor is split from consultative 'supervision' available as consultancy from a non-supervisor. The approach suggested in this text is a flexible model in which consultancy needs are met from a range of sources, one of which is individual sessions with one's supervisor.

In summary, this book is primarily about the activity of seeking and offering consultancy in the context of the continuous professional development of the social worker throughout his career, from student to senior practitioner or manager. Much of this consultancy and related activity actually occurs within the supervisory relationship, so the book is also about the professional component of supervision. The management component is not considered as such, but it is frequently referred to as a central influence on consultancy, whether or not this occurs within supervision. (There are other books on supervision, e.g. Kadushin 1976; Pettes 1979; Westheimer 1977; Shulman 1982, which discuss the administrative aspects comprehensively.)

**Contents**

*Chapter 1* is a framework or map for thinking about consultancy and supervision, and for what follows in later chapters. It begins by defining and distinguishing the two terms, and the related functions of training, staff development and evaluation. The special characteristics of consultancy within a supervisory relationship are discussed, and the importance of agency setting and context are considered. A typology of different models and methods of consultancy, both traditional and innovative, is outlined.

*Chapters 2 and 3* are complementary, focusing on the task, skills and role perspective of the consultee and consultant respectively. Although for clarity of presentation these two roles are considered in separate chapters, the interactional significance of the complete consultee–consultant system, for example in making contracts, the distribution of power, and in games-playing, will be consistently observed, as will the staff group arena in which much of this activity occurs. The influence of supervisory power and authority on supervision-consultation will be discussed.

*Chapter 4* is about the student practice stage. The particular features of the education/training context, compared to the post-qualification employment context, will be outlined, with special attention given to the role of the student in comprehensive preparation for practice placements. The issue of visible practice as an essential part of skill-development and evaluation will be emphasised.

*Chapter 5* outlines the potential and techniques of consultancy in groups. I have written elsewhere (Brown 1979) about groupwork as a mainstream method of work with clients, and the group process can be equally potent in two different kinds of group consultancy. The first is when a group of colleagues (who may be a team as in group supervision) work together on issues arising from their work with clients. The second, which I shall call staff group consultancy, is when a team calls in a consultant to help it resolve issues in its own working relationships (process) and/or programme (task).

*Chapter 6* will place consultancy and supervision in the wider context of an individual's professional development. The different stages will be linked to in-service and post-qualification training provision. The team context and the role of the supervisor will be viewed as central to this process, and as the place where the ambivalences and tensions of the supervisory-consultancy 'equation' need to be worked out.

Finally, the discerning reader may notice at least (!) three biases in the content. These are: toward fieldwork as a setting, toward the CQSW as a training, and toward groups as a social work milieu. I apologise for the first two which reflect the bias of my own work experience rather than a preference. For emphasising the richness of group approaches to both practice and consultancy I make no apology!

# 1 Consultancy and Supervision

There is much confusion in the way the terms consultancy and supervision are used in social work, and it is important (but not easy!) to try and clarify what they each mean, how they overlap, and why the confusion exists. The role distinction is relatively straightforward. A supervisor, usually a line manager, has formally delegated authority over a supervisee, who is directly accountable to her organisationally. A consultant has no formal authority over a consultee who seeks the consultant's help voluntarily. When we come to the functions of consultancy and supervision the confusion begins because in current social work agency practice supervision usually includes consultancy work as a major, or even the main, component, particularly with qualified experienced staff. The confusion increases when we consider supervisory contexts other than the traditional line manager–worker format. For example, in the student practice context, the agency person with overall responsibility for 'supervising' practice placement is variously described as a practice teacher, tutor officer, student supervisor or fieldwork instructor! None of these titles fully describes the multiple functions, one of which is consultancy.

We shall now consider some attempts at definitions:

**Supervision**
Pettes (1979) defines supervision as 'A process by which one social work practitioner enables another social work practitioner who is accountable to her (sic) to practice to the best of his ability.' This definition emphasises the professional, enabling function and seems to imply a one-to-one supervisor–supervisee relationship.

Kadushin (1976) defines supervision in terms of the role and task of the supervisor, and emphasises the managerial function:

> . . . a social work supervisor is an agency administrative staff member to whom authority is delegated to direct, coordinate, enhance, and evaluate on-the-job performance of the supervisees, for whose work he is held accountable . . . The supervisor's ultimate objective is to deliver to agency clients the best possible service, both quantitatively and qualitatively, in accordance with agency policies and procedures.

The relative emphases of these two definitions may to some extent reflect the different historical traditions of supervision in the USA (Kadushin) and the UK (Pettes, also an American but writing about the British context), but varying emphasis on the organisational and professional components of supervision is found throughout social work.

There is general agreement among most writers that supervision has three main functions: *administrative*, *educational* and *supportive*. Like Westheimer (1977) I prefer *managerial* to *administrative* as a more accurate and unequivocal description of the first function. Westheimer also adds a fourth function which she calls *encouraging objectivity*. One of the major functions of a supervisor in practice is to help supervisees to carry out specific pieces of work (whether with individuals, families, groups or communities) as effectively as possible. This function, which has considerable overlap with consultancy, does not seem to be adequately covered by the three elements of management, education and support. Westheimer's 'encouraging objectivity' may have been an attempt to get at this additional function, but although important, 'encouraging objectivity' is only one aspect of this task-focused function of supervision. Prior (1982) refers to a fourth function as the *professional element* of supervision. A team-leader herself, she writes 'there seemed to me to be a major part of supervision connected with the engagement of worker with client which is not directly included in the other (three) elements'. I think what we are identifying here is the consultation function of supervision as it is actually carried out by many supervisors, especially with their more experienced staff.

To summarise, supervision, as currently practised, has four interlocking functions and two overlapping components:

| Functions | Components |
|---|---|
| Managerial/Administrative | |
| Educational | Organisational |
| Supportive | Professional |
| Consultative | |

As stated earlier, this book will concentrate on the professional component, although continually acknowledging and discussing the effects of the management function.

## Consultancy
Consultancy has been defined by Caplan (1970) as:

> The process of interaction between two professional persons — the consultant who is a specialist and the consultee who invokes the consult-

ant's help in regard to current work problems with which he is having some difficulty and which he has decided are within the other's area of specialist competence.

Insley (1959) defined consultation as:

> A helping process which invokes the use of technical knowledge and professional relationships with one or more persons. Its purpose is to help consultees to carry out their professional responsibilities more effectively.

The word 'consultant' has a range of connotations for each of us which, among other things, may influence our willingness to take up either the role of consultant, or consultee, or both, and also influence our behaviour if we do enter a consultancy relationship. Some writers, for example Caplan (1970) write about consultancy in élitist terms to describe the expert, the virtuoso performer. This expertise resides either in the consultant's specialist knowledge about the relevant subject area or in her sophisticated process skills in facilitating problem-solving by the consultee, i.e. process-consultancy, or ideally in both.

By contrast, and more simply, consultancy can be described as any help which one person offers to another who has sought their help and advice, that is, has *consulted* them, *in a professional context*. In this book we are thinking of the whole spectrum of consultancy expertise, ranging from 'the national authority' to 'the local expert' to any colleague, quite possibly someone junior in rank or less experienced, who may be consulted about a particular professional practice issue, and who has a contribution to make to its resolution. I have known many social work students on placement who have been used very successfully for consultation purposes (though rarely is it called that) by qualified experienced workers. We can retain the notion of expertness in consultancy if we wish, but get rid of the élitist connotation by acknowledging that some expertise is present (though not always recognised) in nearly everyone engaged in the social work process, and that includes clients and volunteers. The lower status person rarely attracts the label consultant, or thinks of herself in that role, but that does not invalidate the potential consultative contribution which she can make. That this is not an 'airy-fairy' idea can be seen in the basic premise of social groupwork: that in a group, people sharing similar problems and experiences can offer effective help to one another.

The main theoretical distinctions between supervision and consultancy are summarised in Table 1:

Most of the distinctions are self-explanatory and highlight the main task and role differences. However, the distinction in practice

**Table 1**

| SUPERVISION | CONSULTANCY |
|---|---|
| Compulsory | Voluntary |
| Supervisee accountable to supervisor (usually line-manager) | Freely entered voluntary relationship |
| Supervisor from same profession | Consultant may be from same or related profession |
| Agenda (potentially the whole workload of the supervisee) chosen by the supervisor and supervisee | Agenda chosen by consultee |
| Supervisor is not selected by supervisee, but by role in the organisation | Consultant is selected by consultee on the basis of having the relevant knowledge and skills |
| Decision-making is a shared responsibility | Responsibility for decisions rests with the consultee |
| Continuous activity | Time-limited contract |
| A 'free service' | Sometimes a fee-paying service, or on some negotiated basis |

is not as clear as it is in theory. Supervision, especially for supervisees who are qualified and experienced, is often conducted primarily, or entirely, on a consultancy basis. When this happens, there will nevertheless always be some pressures affecting the consultancy because of the role-relationships in which one is the other's 'boss'. The supervisor carries not only authority but also power over the supervisee—for example to write references, report to senior managers, evaluate work, influence promotion. This managerial/professional duality in supervision is often denied or at least obscured by the participants, but it will always influence the transactions between them, as we shall see when considering the role-relationship of supervisee and supervisor and possible organisational structures for supervision and consultancy.

Conversely, as Kadushin (1977) has shown, when consultancy is offered by a non-supervisor to a consultee employee of an agency, the relationship has not always been entered into freely by the consultee. Others, whether supervisors, co-workers, team-colleagues or management may have been the prime movers in the decision to have a consultant, and in her selection. Nor does the consultant necessarily have no direct influence on decisions taken subsequent to consultation.

*Example:*
A social work agency decided to call in an outside consultant to help develop a new type of groupwork. This consultancy service included individual sessions with pairs of social workers co-leading groups. The majority of these workers were highly motivated to use the consultancy, but one or two felt it had been imposed on them by management, and resisted making good use of it, either by missing appointments or being negative in the sessions.

Before leaving definitions we should mention briefly *evaluation*, *training*, *staff development* and *professional development* because each of these is closely associated, and often overlaps with, consultancy and supervision.

*Evaluation*, in a formal sense, is part of the managerial and educational components of supervision. The supervisor is usually required to evaluate her supervisee's work for agency purposes, and also provide feedback to the supervisee as part of his professional development. The reader is referred to Kadushin (1976, Chapter 5) for a detailed exposition of supervisory evaluation. Evaluation, in an informal sense, is an essential part of good professional practice in which the social worker himself carries responsibility (with help from colleagues, supervisor, consultants and clients) for evaluating his own work.

*Training* is concerned with general organised opportunities for the acquisition of knowledge and skills. Basic or professional training usually refers to courses leading to a professional qualification, with practice 'supervision' as a major component. In-service training is used to describe both comprehensive 'in-house' courses funded by agencies for their unqualified staff, and a range of in-house short courses (usually of a specialist nature) thought to be suitable for the range of 'post-professional' needs of qualified workers.

*Post-qualification* training is a term which has been used in the UK since 1975 to designate medium–long courses approved by CCETSW, and usually offered in educational establishments. It is quite possible that this usage of the term will be extended to reflect the title more accurately by describing the whole gamut of in-house and external shorter and longer courses available to qualified practitioners and managers.

The overlap between training and both supervision and consultancy is considerable. Supervision has the educational function of both direct teaching and facilitation of training opportunities, and consultancy inevitably includes some teaching, training and learning. In the professional model emphasised in this text, the primary responsibility for identification of training needs lies with the worker himself.

*Staff development*, according to Kadushin (1976) is all the procedures that an agency might employ to enhance the job-related knowledge, skills and attitudes of its total staff, and includes in-service training and educational supervision.

*Professional development*, on the other hand, is the individual development of the social worker (or manager), enhancing his professional competence, knowledge and skills, and the quality of his service to clients. Consultancy, as well as the whole spectrum of post-qualifying training, is likely to be a major contributor to an individual's professional development.

**The need for consultancy and supervision**
Consultancy has the potential to improve the quality of every practitioner's and every manager's work, and in that sense all staff need it and can benefit from it throughout their professional careers. (Whether they themselves want it, and whether it is available are different issues!) The need will vary on several dimensions:

(1) *The stage of career-development*
During training and the first two or three years of post-qualification experience (depending in part on pre-training experience, if any) most workers will have a generalised broadly-based need for regular frequent consultancy, much of which is likely to occur within the supervisory relationship. Another need for regular consultancy (although it is not always acknowledged in the same way) arises when a major role-change occurs, such as promotion to team-leader, head-of-home, area director or training officer, or after a transfer to a new agency or setting. As a career progresses in a given role, consultancy needs are likely to become more selective, more specific, and more specialised, and the sources of consultancy are more likely to vary and to be from outside the supervisory relationship.

## (2) The context of agency and setting

In statutory agencies (and some voluntary ones) the accountability and supervisory requirements of the organisation will always profoundly influence consultancy whether or not it comes from the supervisor. Tensions arise as agency requirements are not always seen by practitioners to coincide with the needs of their clients or their own professional development. The more bureaucratically-orientated agency managers may be resistant to the spread of consultancy outside the supervisory relationship, because of the reduced opportunity for direct control and monitoring of worker performance and behaviour. The more professionally-orientated may actively facilitate the development of a range of consultancy sources for their staff.

*Settings.* In traditional fieldwork, social workers make a series of brief episodic interventions into the lives of 'their' clients, most of their work being invisible to colleagues and supervisors. They also work across a complex of agency and community boundaries. In this setting, individual supervision is part of the tradition, but direct information about how the worker actually operates is not. By contrast, in *residential work*, social workers spend many of their working hours with colleagues, in the company of a 'shared' group of clients in a group living context of high visibility to peers, supervisors and others. Human fallibility and the stress of the job are much more difficult to conceal than they are in fieldwork. Yet, as Davis (1982) has commented, individual supervision for residential workers is generally less developed than it is for fieldworkers, although as he points out, with the special stresses and continuous flow of incidents in residential work, the provision of suitable consultancy and supervision for staff is equally important. For more detailed consideration of consultancy in residential work the reader is referred to Davis (1982) and also to an article by Wright (1978) who has produced a useful outline of a supervision model adapted to the particular needs of residential staff. The majority of residential staff who are still unqualified are likely to need more supervisory teaching and direction than their qualified colleagues.

*Day-care* is in a period of rapid expansion and change, as seen in the development of family-centres with a community orientation. As a result, the consultancy needs of day-care staff are still evolving and not well documented. There are however some similarities with the residential setting, for example the open visible context and multi-professional staff groups.

Another setting is what I have referred to (Brown 1979, p.27) rather clumsily as the *non social work orientated institution*, for example hospitals, prisons, schools, in which social workers are often subordinate (in status and role) to other disciplines and professions. In these contexts special features requiring consultancy help are likely to be the social worker's lack of control over his own work context, the uncertain boundaries of role and task, and the demands of interprofessional communication and collaboration often approached from a relatively low-status position. The attachment of social workers to clinical teams in hospitals means membership of two or more work groups, with much scope for team and work system consultancy (see Chapter 5).

(3) *The method of social work being used*
Although the basic principles and skills of consultancy can be applied to all methods of social work, and to those which use integrating frameworks such as the unitary model, differences in social work methods (and client groups) do influence consultancy needs in two important ways. The first and most obvious is the specialist knowledge and skills required; the second is the emotional or process impact which the particular client milieu has on the worker's feelings, and which in turn is mirrored (Mattinson, 1975) or imported into the atmosphere of the consultancy arena. To illustrate this, contrast the feelings a worker is likely to bring when coming to consultancy from: an interview with a depressed individual; a family therapy session fraught with marital and parent-child conflicts; an aggressive challenging peer group of adolescent offenders; and a community residents' meeting pressing the worker to take some controversial action with the local authority.

As you move along the continuum from work with individuals–pairs–families–groups–communities, so the potential complexity of consultancy needs, roles and agendas increases. But this is to over-simplify, because a systemic approach to work with an individual client can involve interventions in a complex of networks which are highly relevant to the consultancy agenda. One important differentiation is those social work approaches which include two or more in the 'worker-system' so that the consultancy agenda has a whole additional area of focus on the role-relationships and management of the worker-system.

Most of the consultancy and supervisory literature implicitly or explicitly refers to the casework method, but a specialist literature has begun to develop for other methods, for example community work (Briscoe 1977), family work (Whiffen and Byng-Hall 1982) and groupwork (Donnellan 1981; Miller 1960). Interesting trends in these developments include family therapists' commitment to various methods of 'live' consultancy (Kingston and Smith 1983), group workers interests in the co-working relationship (Galinsky and Schopler 1980), day-care consultants developing 'on-site' consultancy (Goldschmied 1982), and community work specialists exploring a range of quite active interventionist roles for consultants (Briscoe 1977). A common trend in all this is for consultants to be more actively and directly involved with at least some part of the intervention arena or system. These developments, and features of the different methods, will be referred to in subsequent chapters, but readers wishing to explore any single one in more depth should follow up the sources.

For each of the four methods of social work referred to, and in each of the different settings mentioned, there is a range of possible models, styles, techniques, value-orientations and theoretical approaches, each having significance for both consultancy needs and consultancy skills. To give an obvious example, a behaviourally orientated practitioner working out a programme with a family is likely to need (and want!) consultancy from someone with relevant knowledge, skill and identification with the behavioural approach, and is unlikely to seek it from a psychodynamically inclined or humanistic consultant. Thus consideration of need leads on to issues about consultant selection, style and matching, all of which we shall return to later.

**Sources of consultancy**
The three main sources are: from within the team or immediate staff group; from elsewhere in the consultee's own agency; and from outside the agency.

*Within the team*
The team offers three possible sources of consultancy:
(1) *The line-manager or team-leader*, when consultancy forms part of individual supervision. This has the advantage of being a source of consultancy to which the supervisee is formally entitled as a 'right', whereas most other sources are likely to involve choices, overtures and negotiations. It can also be directly integrated with the oversight and evaluative functions of supervision, although these same assessment-evaluative elements of management may prove a deterrent and source of constraint for the supervisee. Much will depend on the degree of trust and mutual professional respect

between team-member and team-leader, and on whether the latter has the relevant knowledge and skills.

(2) *A team-colleague* offering peer consultancy. This has the practical advantages of high accessibility and convenience, and may also contribute to team cohesion and shared working. Like the supervisor, a colleague will be knowledgeable about the work context and have an established relationship with the consultee. Some possible disadvantages of colleague consultancy are discussed later in the text, including vague agreements, problems of collusion on team or personal 'no-go areas' and a general reluctance to challenge colleagues, e.g. on aspects of a co-working relationship.

(3) *Team-consultancy*, when the team meets together to offer consultancy to individual team-members in a group context. This approach, which may form part of group supervision, requires rather more organisation than the other intra-team sources, but it has considerable potential. Group approaches are discussed in more detail in Chapter 5.

All forms of in-team consultancy have both advantages and disadvantages when compared to sources beyond the team, and they are not of course mutually exclusive. Teams and team-members who do not seek any form of consultancy stimulus from beyond their own boundaries may risk becoming rather incestuous and inward-looking in style, and restricted in their knowledge and skill repertoire.

*Elsewhere in the agency*

Many of the larger agencies have a number of consultancy type posts which are outside operational line-management and which are usually associated with either a client group, for example the physically handicapped, or a method of working, for example groupwork, or both, for example intermediate treatment. The holders of these posts, which may be at headquarters or area level, have an array of titles including adviser, development officer and consultant. Rowbottom and Bromley (1980 Chapter 8) distinguish between *specialist development officers* who carry agency-wide responsibility for the general development of a specialist service and *consultant practitioners* who retain a practice function and are mainly involved in consultancy to particular workers and projects. The Stevenson–Parsloe study (1978) found, to nobody's surprise, that they were often under-used, except when the consultant or specialist had former personal connections with the team.

Another possibility is the unofficial use of colleagues in the agency who have relevant expertise or specialist knowledge, which are known about in the the informal networks but who have no designation or authority which recognises them in any formal way. This means that a potentially fruitful source of consultancy is often negated by boundary-crossing problems, administrative complications, and uncertainty about the agency mandate of such a person to offer consultancy, and of another to seek it. These are obstacles which can be overcome by persistence, flexibility and negotiating skills but a comment in the Stevenson–Parsloe study (1978, p.209) is pertinent: 'Help and advice did not come exclusively from within the team, but examples of social workers seeking other forms of support were exceedingly limited . . . For the vast majority of those we inteviewed, their work world comprised their team and their clients.' That was true for a sample of Social Services Department teams in 1975–7. There are some indications that developments in training programmes and worker sophistication since then have increased the use of consultancy from beyond the boundaries of the team, but still as the exception rather than the rule. I suspect that apart from the logistical obstacles, some resistance is in both management (fearing that line-management control will be undermined) and workers (lack of energy and confidence in being proactive in seeking consultancy resources). Ways of overcoming these obstacles are needed because with increasingly well-qualified, skilled and experienced staff there is a vast underused consultancy potential among the practitioners in most agencies and settings. With limited opportunities for promotion, and little expansion of specialist posts, this is the major consultancy resource of the future. Just as it has been important to shift from the individual worker to the team concept, so it is now necessary to take a multi-team perspective, at least in resource terms.

*Outside the agency*
The external or 'outside' consultant is likely to be selected because of some recognised expertise and skill which she has, and which may not be available in the agency, or when there are some strong reasons for having an independent person. Quite often such a person is known personally or by reputation, and part of the attraction is the confidentiality offered when unburdening and perhaps disclosing vulnerability and uncertainty to an independent trusted person. Also, a fresh knowledge, skill and attitude perspective may be expected. On the other hand, such people have to be found, negotiated with, probably paid, and they may not know

much about the consultee's work context. As we shall see in Chapter 5, an effective and economical use of the external consultant is for a whole team, staff group or work unit to seek consultancy on some aspect of its work programme or on its own work system's functioning. Another use of an outside consultant is to facilitate an innovation or new method of working, as a base from which the agency can develop its own internal expertise and future consultancy resource.

**Types of consultancy**
This typology draws to some extent on those developed by others (especially Watson 1973), whilst attempting to provide a more comprehensive range which takes into account current developments, particularly those approaches in which the consultant is present in some role during the actual intervention. The models are divided between those in which:
(1) the consultant is *not* present at the time of the practice intervention, termed *non-participant consultancy*;
(2) the consultant *is* present in some *active* role for at least part of the actual intervention, termed *participant consultancy*; and
(3) those when the consultant has firsthand information, but does not get actively involved at the time, termed *observed consultancy*.

*Non-participant consultancy*
(1) *The tutorial*. This is the classical one-to-one consultancy, with the consultant in the non-reciprocal role of 'expert' and/or supervisor. If two (or more) are working together as in conjoint marital work or co-leadership of a group, then the format will be 1:2+, as it is unsatisfactory, although sometimes unavoidable, to have consultancy with only part of the 'worker-system'.
(2) *Tandem, peer–pair consultancy*. This is another one-to-one model, but occurring between similarly experienced workers consulting with one another on a mutually reciprocal basis, though not necessarily concurrently. The two participants may or may not be part of the same work-group. An example would be worker A being consultant to worker B about his work with family X this month, and worker B becoming consultant to worker A about his work with family Y next month. A counselling analogue of this model is co-counselling (Heron 1978) in which the terms client rather than consultee, and counsellor rather than consultant are used to describe the reciprocal roles of the two partners whose agendas and methods are personal rather than professional. Despite the

difference in aims and content, some of the basic principles and processes, for example that the primary responsibility for the session rests with 'the client', and the requirement that the counsellor be a good listener, affirm the worth of the other, and provide a secure supportive environment, are important for peer–pair consultancy, as indeed they are for all forms of effective helping.

Not all peer–pair consultancy is necessarily exclusive to a tandem. Variations include peer consultancy in a wider network of reciprocity between several peers, for example A to B, B to C, C to A, D to B, E to C, A to E and so on. Another variation is when two pairs of co-workers offer consultancy to each other. This is not the same as peer group consultancy because only two work units are involved, and the roles of consultant and consultee are not necessarily exchangeable within the session.

(3) *Facilitated group consultancy*. This occurs when a group of workers meets together for consultancy, with a facilitator in a distinct and separate role. The potential agenda will include issues arising from the several quite distinct, although sometimes similar, work episodes of the different workers represented. The facilitator's task is to enable the group, including herself, to provide effective consultancy for individuals (or pairs) who present issues. In this model, all group members take a quasi-consultant role except when they are presenting their work from a consultee role. This, and the other group models below, are discussed in more detail in Chapter 5.

(4) *Group supervision* is a particular version of facilitated group consultancy, the distinction being that the facilitator is the supervisor (selection by role), the members are all, or some, of her supervisees (again, selection by role), and the agenda will be influenced by managerial as well as professional criteria.

Some versions of group supervision have the designated leadership rotating, which raises issues about the supervisor's role and how accountability is exercised.

(5) *Peer group consultancy*, a group version of tandem consultancy, is a self-help model, the emphasis being on reciprocity, self-help and interchangeability of roles. This model is particularly effective with experienced workers doing similar work.

*Participant consultancy models*

A number of variations of this model are possible:

(6) *Joint work*. This is when the consultant and consultee (or

perhaps more often the supervisor and supervisee) work together with an individual, family, group or community. The difference from other forms of joint work is that this is a type of apprenticeship model in which the distinct roles of the two workers are defined, so that whilst there is some mutuality of learning, the consultee gets consultancy help from the consultant as they work together, as well as in preparation beforehand and review afterwards. It is different from 'live' consultancy because the consultant is working actively and directly with the clients. Sometimes the two workers may have differentiated tasks with the same client system, as in one example when a practice teacher worked primarily with the single parent father, and his student worked solely with his seven children. The practice teacher retained overall responsibility for the welfare of the children. (See Weekes, Osborn and Holgate 1977).

(7) *Live consultancy*. In this model, much favoured by family therapy specialists, the consultant is present throughout the work session, but in a consultant role only. Her primary task is to enable the worker to help the clients more effectively, *during the session, as the work is continuing*. She does this by periodic advice, comments (and sometimes instructions) and by the use of short periods of 'time-out' which can be called on by either the consultant or consultee when they withdraw briefly for interval consultation. This model includes a preparatory session beforehand and a review afterwards. There are two principal versions of this model (see Whiffen and Byng-Hall 1982):

(i) *consultancy from behind a one-way screen*; and
(ii) *consultancy in the same room*.

When a one-way screen is used, the consultant or consultants (sometimes a consultancy team) are invisible, but able to observe the proceedings. She/they communicate with the consultee by telephone or ear-plug, and on occasions may enter the room to make an intervention. When ear-plug or telephones are used the clients do not hear the consultant's comments, although with a telephone they know they are being made.

Consultancy in the same room (Smith and Kingston 1980; Kingston and Smith 1983) has the consultant sitting a little back from the consultee and the client group, and in some versions comments or actions may be made by the consultant directly to the participants, as well as to the consultee, which of course they also hear. The more that comments are made directly to the participants, the more similar to joint work the approach becomes.

The respective merits of the two versions are debated elsewhere (Smith and Kingston 1980), but for most practitioners except those in specialist psychiatric or family therapy settings the 'same room' version will be the most practicable one, as no special resources are needed. Live consultancy approaches can be used by peer–pair consultants (switching roles for different clients) or by supervisor with supervisee as a training model. Aside from work with families, these methods can be used with groups. There are reservations though, about their use with individuals, as there is some evidence (Ainley and Kingston 1981) of the client feeling intimidated.

Although this model is distinguished from 'joint work', it can legitimately be viewed as a structured form of co-working with ascribed roles.

(8) *Periodic 'on-site' consultancy*. Another development is when the consultant is physically present, either in the room, or else close by, during *selected* periods of the work being done. Her task is to help the consultee both indirectly by interval consultancy, and directly by participating in the action to demonstrate or role-model a particular helping behaviour. She may also intervene in a crisis. One exponent of this method is a day-nursery consultant (Goldschmied 1982) who periodically observes the work being done, discusses techniques with the staff, on site, and at other times actively enters the nursery arena to, say, demonstrate a particular form of play-therapy with a child. Another example is an intermediate-treatment consultancy service (Errington and Feeny 1981) which, whilst working mostly in a non-participant mode, uses the opportunity of the residential weekend part of the IT programme, held at the consultancy centre, to make selected consultancy interventions both with staff and by modelling work with the adolescent group. Residential and day-care settings are both particularly well suited to this approach, but it also has considerable potential in fieldwork.

In all these participant models it is essential that clients as well as workers have a clear understanding of the consultant's role, its boundaries and flexibility, and the nature of the relationship between the consultant and the clients.

While it seems unlikely that participant or 'live' models will become the norm outside of the specialist sophisticated settings where they have been mostly developed (apart from anything else they are more expensive in resources), there is much potential for their increased use and particularly in the early stages of a social worker's career when some experience of first-hand consultancy and supervision, with the insight it gives to personal style and method, is so important.

### 'Observed' or 'direct evidence' consultancy

This is an intermediate model where the consultant has first-hand information about the work session(s), but only intervenes with the consultee before and after the live work. The information can be obtained either by direct non-participant observation of the work (in the room, at the meeting, or invisibly through a screen), or by video- or audio-tape-recordings of the event. Tapes are really techniques or resources, which can be used to make non-participant consultancy more authentic.

### Selection of consultancy source and type

Having clarified the range of sources and types of consultancy, the question of selection for a particular consultancy need now arises. Figure 1 indicates some key variables associated with consultancy *need* (Box 1) and sets them alongside the range of *sources* of consultancy (Box 2) and *types* of consultancy (Box 3). Whilst this in itself will not help the prospective consultee with the actual selection of source and type, it does indicate the range of potential choices available. Many factors will influence and constrain actual choice, including agency expectations, feasibility, attitudes, anticipated benefits and individual preferences. Because of this complexity and the limited state of our knowledge of consultancy and its evaluation, it is not possible or appropriate to give clear guidelines for matching need, source and type. It is hoped, however, that the more detailed discussion in the following chapters will contribute to the making of choices and to creative developments in consultancy, both in and out of supervision.

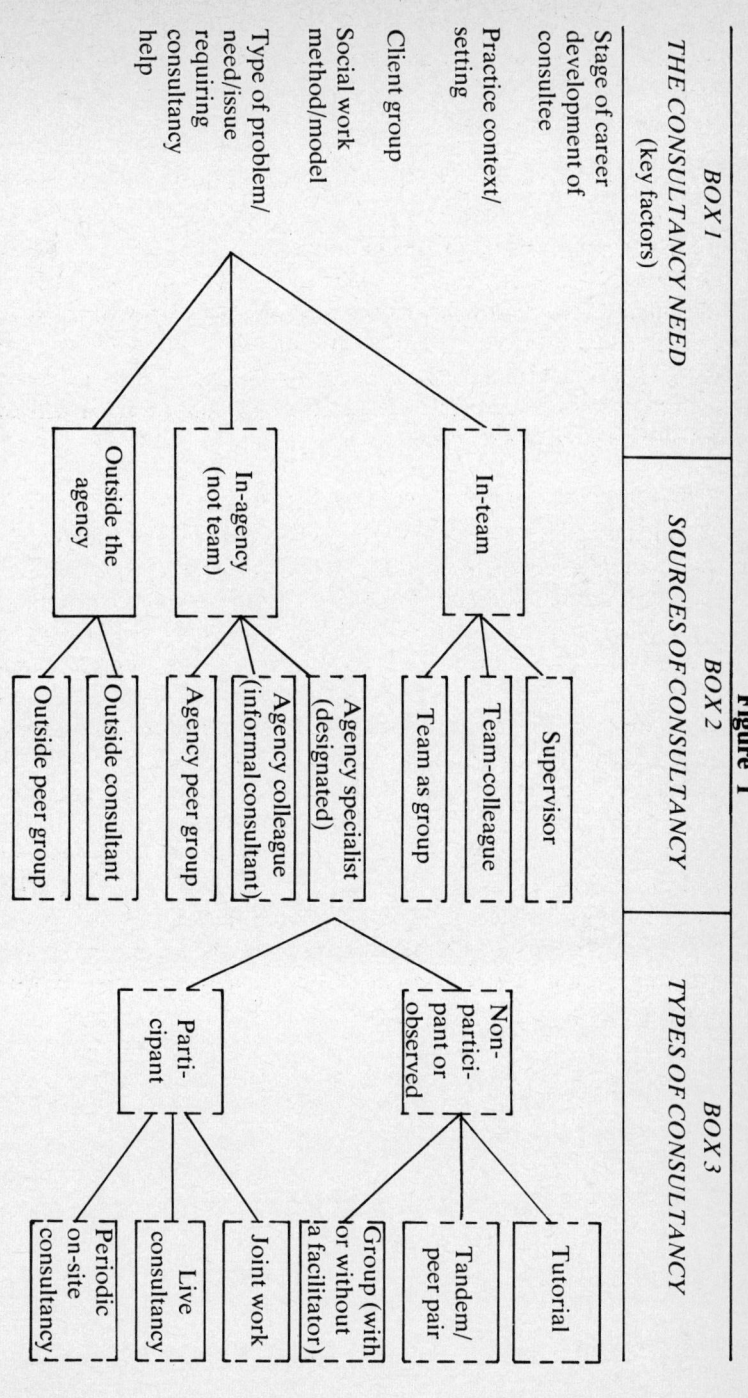

**Figure 1**

# 2 The Consultee

This chapter differs from most of the literature on consultancy and supervision because it is concerned with the often neglected role, perspective and skills of the consultee/supervisee (*note*: consultee is used except when the supervisory context is significant). Nearly all the available information is about what the supervisor or consultant should do, reflecting perhaps the pedagogic and managerial orientations of social work education and practice respectively. The implication that the consultee is a somewhat passive responder to the initiatives of others is unfortunate, and to redress the balance the focus here will be specifically on the interests and skills of the consultee, who is viewed as an active initiator and participant in consultancy and supervision transactions.

We shall consider first the stance and needs of the consultee, and then how these needs vary according to his stage of career development. This will be followed by a section on the self-monitoring and development of learning and work styles, as these are seen as basic to the consultee's orientation and approach. Next is a core section on the consultancy process itself, offering a consultee perspective on preparation, contract and the consultancy session. The final section considers the consultee role in different types of consultancy, and in supervision in particular.

## Basic stance and needs

The quality of professional help available to the worker varies with the organisational context and accessibility of resources, but equally important is the stance, attitude and initiative taken by the consultee himself. It is easy, as so often happens when there is dissatisfaction with the quality of professional support, to blame the supervisor, the agency or the workload. Even in apparently adverse circumstances, there is much that the consultee can negotiate and achieve himself if he is prepared to accept that *he* is primarily responsible for his own professional development, and, together with colleagues and senior staff, for obtaining the consultancy and other resources he needs. This approach requires the qualified worker to be skilled in 'identifying his own areas of competence, partial ability and limitation' (Scherz 1958), and in assessing the composite of his own knowledge, skills and personal style. The philosophy of self-learning and self-development will be familiar to readers of Rogers (1961) and Freire (1970), and is also consistent with some contemporary trends in social work practice which emphasise the client's active participation in his own learning.

Some information is available (Parsloe and Hill 1978; Satyamurti 1981; Kadushin 1974; Hughes 1980) about what supervisees would like from supervision, and about their satisfactions and dissatisfactions with what they actually get. Information about consultees' views is very scarce (but see Kadushin 1977), perhaps because consultancy *per se* occurs so much less frequently than supervision. However, much consultancy occurs within the supervisory relationship, so information drawn from that source can provide useful indications of consultee expectations. What emerges from these studies, and from my own contacts with numerous social workers, is a confused situation with some clear pointers identifiable. The confusion is of two kinds. Firstly, a lack of clarity about the purpose, content and nature of consultancy and supervision, appears in the conflicting expectations of consultees, supervisors and agency. The second area of confusion comes from the ambivalence of the worker himself about seeking help with work-related problems. On the one hand there is a need to share with others the pressures and problems of a difficult demanding job, but on the other there are the risks of self-exposure, judgement by others, and the challenge to change, or at least modify, established practices. In a job in which the criteria of success and failure are often complex and ill-defined, the worker is perhaps particularly dependent on, and vulnerable to, the judgements of others.

In the midst of this confusion, some clear pointers emerge from the studies. The worker is looking for three main types of help which overall rank about equal in importance, varying in priority according to circumstances such as stage of career development. *The first is an opportunity to reflect on problems being encountered in work with clients, and to discuss practical ways of solving them, including help with important decision-making.* This was rated highest in the American consultancy study, but it is also very prominent in studies of supervisees. It usually refers to specific 'client' (individual, family, group, or community) problems with which the worker is involved. It is the area of consultative problem-solving which I referred to as the fourth function of supervision (see p.2). The second type of help is *the need for support and the sharing of the 'burden' of a very demanding and responsible job*. This need is specific in relation to a particular piece of work or source of stress, and general in relation to the worker's need for personal valuation and positive feedback. This latter need which is not always felt by social workers to be legitimate or respectable, is sometimes underestimated by management. Perhaps for this last reason it is a difficult one to express without appearing to show weakness (in fact it is often a sign of strength to be able to acknowledge such a need). The third type of help rated highly by workers is *help with general development as a professional worker*. This is more difficult to define precisely, but it refers to improvement in overall competence, skills and knowledge, and includes various types of training provision as well as any direct contribution from consultancy sessions. Other important needs mentioned, such as workload management and advice on procedures, resources and information, fall within the managerial-administrative function of supervision.

Dissatisfactions expressed by workers are primarily associated with the non-fulfilment of one or more of these three primary needs of problem-solving, support and professional development. They also include criticism of 'irregular', 'unreliable', 'ignorant' and 'non-challenging' supervision.

Awareness of these needs and sources of dissatisfaction is important information for all managers, supervisors and consultants who are concerned to improve both staff morale and standards of practice. In this chapter we concentrate on what the worker himself can do to try and ensure that his consultancy needs are met.

## Stages of career development

The social worker's need for consultancy and supervision will vary in type, source and frequency according to his level of experience. Five different career stages can be identified and related to consultancy need.

*Pre-professional* This stage, which includes unqualified and voluntary work undertaken prior to professional training, is not covered in this text. Many of the general principles of self-directed learning skills apply, but the need for basic information and teaching is greater, and the boundaries between consultancy, supervision and training are blurred.

*Professional training–the student stage* The importance of the practice placement supervision experience cannot be overstated, particularly for students with no previous experience of regular supervision. This is an impressionable time when patterns are set that can orientate and shape future consultancy habits, expectations and attitudes. Much of this chapter is directly relevant to the student role, and in Chapter 4 we shall discuss specific ways of preparing actively for practice placements and being a student supervisee. The practice teacher who will be, whether intentionally or not, a role-model for the student has a big responsibility, but so has the student who can contribute so much to his own learning.

*First two years, post-qualification* The first year of this formative period is marked formally in the Probation Service as being subject to confirmation, and if the recommendation of the Barclay Report (1982) is adopted, a probationary year will be required in all agencies, with the professional qualification depending on the successful completion of the first year in post as well as the training course itself. Whether or not it is formally recognised in this way it is a period when working patterns are set, roles adopted and approaches to supervision and consultation established. The newly qualified worker is inevitably quite dependent on his supervisor, but whether this relationship is based on acquiescence or a negotiated contract rests as much in the hands of the worker as the supervisor.

*Two–five years, post-qualification* This is a critical period in a social worker's development. The two-year point is marked by eligibility for both supervising student placements and attending formal post-qualification courses approved by CCETSW. The practitioner is consolidating a basic professional competence, and is beginning to develop specific areas of expertise, though still with much to learn. A primary source of his learning will be through consultancy which he is now increasingly likely to negotiate for in specific terms, whether with his supervisor or from elsewhere. Those writers (e.g. Hollis 1964) who advocate a time-limit for professional supervision for qualified staff suggest the four–six year period as the turning point.

*Five years plus, post-qualification* At this stage the worker will be developing further, perhaps as a senior practitioner, or in some specialist post, or in some new role, say in middle management. He may now be regarded as quite an expert in particular areas of skill and knowledge, and be used frequently as a consultant himself, but this does not remove his own need for consultancy on both his direct practice and consultancy practice. This help will be sought more selectively, and peer models are likely to be both congenial and useful at this stage.

Middle-managers and team leaders also need consultancy to help them with their difficult and responsible jobs, not least to improve the quality of the supervisory and consultancy resources they offer to social workers.

## Styles of learning and working

An essential skill for all consultees is the ability to identify and monitor their own *learning-style* and *work-style*. People vary considerably in their 'natural' styles, whilst each individual's basic approach may not change radically over time, there is much scope for development over the career span. A person's style 'baseline', whether assessed at the beginning of professional training, and/or at later stages in his career serves both as a reminder of the influence of past experiences on present functioning, and more optimistically, as a guide to development and progress in the future.

### *Learning style*

The *active learner* is a person who actively takes responsibility for how and what he learns, both in the sphere of knowledge and understanding, and in his work behaviour and skills. To be an active learner requires having some idea about how you learn best and which learning skills you need to develop, in order to establish your learning baseline as a basis for planning your future learning goals and directions.

Learning patterns are shaped by a combination of individual factors, intellectual potential, parental or family influences, approaches experienced in formalised learning contexts, for example schools, colleges, and the whole range of life experiences in leisure and work activity. This background will determine a person's position on a passive-active learning continuum. The 'passive' end is characterised by a reliance on instruction and the example of others, a 'teacher knows best' approach in which the individual is highly dependent on didactic teaching and imitative learning. The 'active' end is characterised by the independent original stance of a person who has probably been encouraged and rewarded for exploratory inquisitive self-discovery and risk-taking learning. Alternatively, some independent learners may have developed their approach as a direct reaction against a prescriptive authoritarian upbringing and/or education. Independent thinkers and 'doers' with this type of background may have particular problems about accepting that they have anything to learn from teachers who are in any position of authority. By contrast, the effective active learner is a person who, whilst taking responsibility for his own learning, is also able to make the best possible use of all the learning resources available to him, including consultancy help from supervisor, colleagues and outside specialists.

## How we learn
Before briefly exploring the range of learning styles, we should note that when faced with a new learning requirement in an area of knowledge and/or behaviour that is quite new, most people go through several recognised stages which Bertha Reynolds (1965) identified, chronologically, as:
(1) Acute consciousness of self,
(2) Sink-or-swim adaptation,
(3) Understanding the situation without power to control one's own activity in it,
(4) Relative mastery, in which one can both understand and control one's own activity in the art which is learned, and
(5) Learning to teach what one has mastered.

The student social worker will surely recognise the validity of these stages (which do not necessarily follow in a smooth progression), as will the newly-qualified worker, the recently appointed team-leader, the first-time lecturer, and the occupier of any new and unfamiliar role. I would add one qualification to viewing the fifth stage as the last. Teaching others is an excellent way of learning, and this is another reason for encouraging relatively inexperienced pre-mastery people to contribute to the consultancy of others, for what they will gain as well as contribute. This should not of course be at the expense of the consultee's own learning or the needs of his clients.

Despite these common elements, different people do learn in very different ways. For example:
(1) The *'deep-end'* approach of leaping in and *doing* first, then reflecting afterwards.
(2) *'Sitting by Nelly'* in which the learner observes the 'master' doing the job, and subsequently imitates the observed role-model.
(3) The *apprenticeship model* in which the learner is closely prepared, observed, and trained by the 'master'.
(4) The *'thinker'* who spends a long time preparing, mostly on his own, before reaching a carefully thought out approach to the task.
(5) The *'talker'* who learns best by communicating and interacting verbally with others, individually and in groups.
(6) The *'writer'* who likes to write things down and 'think on paper'.
(7) The *'reader'* who reads extensively on the subject as his main preparation (the theory equivalent of 'sitting by Nelly').
(8) The *'rehearser'* who engages in experiential activities, like simulations, role-plays and rehearsals of the real thing.

These methods, some of which are not of course mutually exclusive, are all valid ways of learning. Knowing which works best for you is important information for your approach to new learning, for capitalising on your current style and strengths, but also to add to your repertoire by training yourself in other methods for which you have some motivation. To give a personal example, my 'natural' style is to learn through interaction with others, both in discussion and experientially, supported by reading. This approach has its limitations when trying to write a book like this one! I have therefore had to try and train myself in reflective thinking and in the use of writing to organise my thoughts and clarify my understanding to a point where I can communicate usefully through the written word, as well as through interpersonal contact which I prefer and find easier. It is for the reader to judge whether I have been successful in this(!), but undoubtedly it has extended my learning repertoire. Readers who would like a fuller discussion of learning and teaching in the context of social work supervision are referred to Westheimer's useful chapter (1977, Chapter 5).

There are two main ways of identifying your own learning style: through self-assessment; and through feedback from others, including peers, trainers, tutors, supervisors and consultants. Priestley, McGuire et al. (1978) outline a useful model of self-assessment in their book on social skills training. The essence of the approach is that the 'student', aided by various paper-and-pencil exercises, sentence completion, 'snakes' and 'ladders', self-ratings and so on, and with the help of peer counselling, feedback and group discussion, makes more conscious what he already knows about his own approach to learning, and the knowledge and skills he already has. This assessment is then used as a springboard for setting objectives, learning new skills and evauation. Adapted versions of this model are used in 'self-positioning' programmes on social work training courses and have been found very useful (see Chapter 4).

**Work-style**

Some years ago I wrote an article 'Worker-Style in Social Work' (Brown 1977) which evoked considerable interest among social work teams and individuals. Aside from introspective curiosity, people have found the concept of personal work-style reassuring because it legitimises differences between workers without passing a value-judgement on their relative merits, helps a staff-group assess their combined resources and skills, and an individual to 'own' and accept his *actual* (as distinct from his *imagined*) style. Paradoxically this 'ownership' can free him to develop and extend his style repertoire in new directions. An interesting example of this from the world of football appeared in an *Observer* article (McIlvanney, 18.11.79) about Brian Clough's approach as a manager to one of his players, 'Take John Robertson. I had to overcome a barrier with him. He's a little fat lad . . . But once you've got him to accept that, you can go on to say he is one of the best deliverers of a ball in the game today . . . but there is no way he is going to get the most out of that fact unless he accepts the other.'

Understanding your own work-style is an important part of being an effective consultee because it helps you to understand how you interact and behave when working with others (whether colleagues, clients, volunteers, supervisor, consultant or other professionals). This is the baseline for skill development, and one of the ingredients of effective consultancy is feedback to the consultee on his style. If such feedback is not forthcoming, it needs to be asked for by the active consultee.

Space does not permit a detailed examination of work-style, but some of the most important dimensions and continua of consultee style are:

(1) *Task/Process* Are you primarily concerned with effectiveness and achieving the task, or with the relationships, feelings, and interactions of the participants (=process)? Or do you give equal attention to both? (See Johnson and Johnson 1975, Chapter 2, for a test on this.) Your task-process orientation is important because it will influence the focus of work with clients and the approach to interactions with supervisors and consultants. You may want a consultant with a similar inclination to your own, for example matched task emphasis, or alternatively, one who presses you to consider the dimensions you tend to ignore, pointing out to the relationship-orientated worker his tendency to forget the purpose of the work, and to the task-orientated worker how, in his enthusiasm to solve the problem, he underestimates what other people are feeling and experiencing during the process.

(2) *Structured/Unstructured* Is your approach to your work relatively structured or unstructured? This will influence your approach to both practice and consultancy. For example, if you like things to be clearly structured and planned, you may have trouble communicating well with a consultant who works on a 'free association' or 'let's see what comes up' basis.

(3) *Theoretical/Values framework*  Do you have an attachment to a particular theoretical framework, be it psychoanalytic, behavioural, humanistic, strategic, structural or systemic, and/or to a particular belief system, be it Christian, Humanistic, Marxist or Zen-Buddhist? Such attachments are basic to a consultee's approach to social work and a source of potential conflict in consultancy.

(4) *Self-disclosing/Non self-disclosing*  Is your natural style to reveal much about yourself in your work (whether unintentionally, or deliberately as a practice skill), or to keep personal disclosures to a minimum? This will also affect consultancy.

> *Example:*
> Recently, as consultant, I disclosed something about my own experience as a divorcee to two social workers leading a group for divorced people. It transpired later that one of them found my disclosure to be unexpected if not inappropriate, and subsequent discussion revealed that he rarely used self-disclosure in either his social worker or consultant roles. Our contrasting styles on self-disclosure affected our communication and his capacity to use what I had hoped was a facilitating contribution.

(5) *Reaction to stress*  How do you react to stress, and what strategies do you use for its management? Fight or flight, withdrawal, denial, confrontation, psychosomatic complaints or rational problem-solving?

(6) *Working with individuals, families, groups, communities*  Which of these ways of working attracts you, and which do you feel least suited to? Experience has shown the value of building on existing strengths and developing skills in less 'natural' areas. Consultancy may be particularly valuable in extending style flexibility and repertoire.

> *Example:*
> One student who saw herself as an introverted one-to-one worker, was very frightened of groups when she started her training course — on a practice placement with good supervision she 'risked' some groupwork, and later became very confident in that method.

(7) *Types of people and problems*  How does your aptitude for working with people vary according to their sex, age, ethnicity, personality, and their manifest problems such as handicap, illness, offending, parenting and poverty? Difficulties of congruence or compatability may be identified and worked at in consultancy.

(8) *Social work tasks and skills* How does your motivation and aptitude vary for different basic tasks and skills such as assessment, advocacy, liaison, enabling, counselling, problem-solving, and the use of authority? Is this affecting the problem on which you are seeking consultancy, and your motivation to seek it?

*Useful methods of identifying personal work style*
*Personal reflection*, and note-taking on your own behaviour and attitudes. Suitable questionnaires and paper-and-pencil exercises can assist this process.
*Personal feedback* from audio or video recordings of your own behaviour.
*Feedback from colleagues* in the team, staff- or student-group.
*Feedback from consultants, supervisors and trainers.*
*Experiential games*, exercises role-plays and simulations in which characteristic and sometimes unexpected behaviours are manifest.

> *Example:*
> Some radical social work students organised the star-power game at a conference workshop. Some participants challenged the game's rules and the authority of the leaders, who became increasingly authoritarian and ruthless in their management of the 'deviants'. When reviewing the workshop subsequently they confessed to being amazed at their own behaviour which did not fit their avowed principles. This was an important, if painful piece of learning about *actual* as distinct from *professed* style, and of how behaviour can change under pressure.

One effect of this baselining on learning and work-styles is that it often stimulates a heightened awareness and capacity for self-monitoring, so that the worker develops a new level of sensitivity and consciousness about his own work behaviour. This will improve the quality of his work, and his awareness of how consultancy can be used to best advantage.

A final point on work-style is that it will profoundly affect a worker's enthusiasm or otherwise for consultancy and the consultee role. For example, an open sharing style is likely to correlate with enthusiastic consultancy-seeking, and conversely a 'private' individualistic style to be associated with consultancy-avoidance.

**Preparation for consultancy**
The section that follows is based on the assumption that consultancy is likely to be particularly effective when it is based on *anticipated* need and is carefully planned and contracted. We should note, however, that in practice there is often a need for immediate *ad hoc*

or *crisis* consultancy. In these circumstances the consultee will seek informal advice from whoever is around, an approach that is particularly common in residential work and in fieldwork teams with open-plan offices. A rather different need, for *'midstream'* consultancy arises when a piece of work which has been continuing for some time becomes stuck or especially difficult. The consultee then seeks help on a planned 'one-off' or sessional basis. Much supervisory consultancy occurs in this way. The processes which are discussed below for planned anticipated consultancy mostly apply also to midstream consultancy, but inevitably in the latter case, the preparatory stages are likely to be short-circuited as time is at a premium.

## Selection of Consultant

The consultee needs to select a consultant in whom he has confidence and with whom he expects to be able to work effectively. Theoretically, the choice is almost unlimited, including supervisor, team-colleagues, senior practitioners, official and unofficial specialists elsewhere in the agency, and outsiders. In practice the choice is likely to be constrained in various ways. The supervisor may wish to undertake most of the consultancy herself, particularly with recently qualified workers. In *ad hoc* and crisis consultancy, there is a need to find someone urgently and this is likely to mean supervisor or immediate colleagues, who are usually the most accessible. Another problem is knowing *who* there is elsewhere in the agency, or outside it, with the necessary skills and interest. If the proposed consultant is an outsider there may be a fee to pay, and if she is an insider she, as well as the consultee, may have negotiations to conduct with interested third parties such as their respective supervisors.

These potential barriers to choice often deter the prospective consultee who may not even bother to test for feasibility. *A basic consultee skill is actively negotiating for the consultancy you need.* This requires knowing what you want, why you want it, and what is potentially available. It also means negotiating in a firm, convincing and authoritative manner, whilst recognising sensitively the implications for others, not least the supervisor. Large hierarchical organisations often appear as formidable barriers to practitioners who understandably often underestimate their power to influence their own working environment. However, when professional credibility is established and a convincing case is made that service to clients will be improved, the case for resources, such as consultancy fees, is very strong. This is not mere theorising (!) as I know of many examples where workers have successfully negotiated for an outside consultant (often for some new piece of work, say a parent effectiveness group, some family therapy, a community based social work approach or a new day-centre), and other instances where people complain but do not test the possibilities. Regarding intra-agency consultation, or any consultation when no payment is involved, it is a moot point whether an experienced qualified worker needs to ask anyone's permission. He is a professional person, fully responsible for his own work, and beyond the courtesy of informing his supervisor and ensuring that accountability is covered satisfactorily, he should be free to make his own arrangements for the resources he needs.

When staff groups really function as a team with sharing of needs, tasks and policy, issues surrounding selection of consultants, the terms on which consultancy occurs, and the tie-up with supervision, will naturally form part of team business. This is a preferred model (to be discussed in more detail in the final chapter) but always subject to the proviso that the needs of the individual worker do not become totally submerged in the collective.

Practitioners often say, 'I/We need a consultant but who on earth is there who knows about this and would be interested to help?' It is indeed difficult for an individual to assemble this information, and it is part of the collective responsibility of teams, special-interest groups, agency management and others to collate and disseminate information about suitable people, internal and external. An American study (Kadushin 1977) showed that a common pattern was for people to approach someone with whom they already had, currently or previously, a work relationship (perhaps as tutor, colleague, senior or a workshop acquaintance). My experience is that people frequently use these networks of contacts. The alternative is to select someone who is known as an authority on her subject through writings, research, practice or past consultancy.

When consultee(s) and potential consultant are strangers, it is a sensible precaution to postpone confirmation of an agreement to work together until after a first meeting which in addition to clarifying expectations, task and arrangements, is also a testing ground for the future work-relationship and *modus operandi*.

## Contract

Any consultancy (including supervision consultancy), other than crisis or one-off sessions, needs to be set up on an agreed basis, preferably written down after negotiations. The consultee (or if two or more workers are involved, then collectively) needs to approach this meeting clear about the limits of negotiability, and with ideas formulated, but not necessarily set, in the following areas:

(1) *Purpose, focus and methods to be used* This includes the clarification of consultee(s) and consultant expectations, and their role-relationship.
(2) *Confidentiality* of information and behaviour disclosed in consultancy sessions.
(3) *Accountability* arrangements, and the consultant's relationship (if any) with the worker's line-manager and relevant others, for example team-colleagues.
(4) *Clients'* relationship, if any, with the consultant. In participant models this is central and a tripartite client–consultee–consultant agreement may be needed.
(5) *Preparation* expected for consultancy sessions, for example advance submission of recorded material.
(6) *Practical and administrative arrangements*, for example location, number, length and frequency of meetings, fees and expenses (if any).
(7) *Provision for evaluation and review*, both of the relevant piece of work, and of the consultancy itself.

Some aspects need further comment:

*Multi-worker consultancy* When two or more workers collaborate in the same project, they should all be involved in the same consultancy sessions. Exceptionally, when this is not possible, for example due to rotas in residential work, clear understanding is needed of how the consultancy work with part of the worker system is to be communicated to the absentees, and ways found of dealing with issues of continuity and exclusion/inclusion.

*Purpose* In consultancy, the consultee(s) decides the purpose although he may wish to have discussion on this with the prospective consultant. In supervision-consultancy both contribute and any real or imagined hidden agendas about purpose need to be 'out on the table' at the contract stage, for example is it part of worker evaluation?

*Focus* The consultee(s) should indicate to the consultant whether he/they want the focus to be consultee-centred, client-centred, programme-centred, context-centred or unrestricted. It is not uncommon, particularly in supervision, for workers to complain that they sought help with client problems and found that their own difficulties became the prime target of interest. This kind of uncertainty and ambiguity is less likely when the issue is discussed openly.

*Methods* It is useful to have some general indication in advance of the methods/techniques which the consultant plans to use. If consultees have strong preferences for, or dislikes of, particular techniques, for example sculpting, role-play, video, it is helpful to say so at this stage.

*Confidentiality* It is important that the consultee clarifies with the consultant whether confidentiality will be partial or absolute, and what will actually happen in practical terms. Absolute confidentiality means that no information about anything that takes place in the consultancy sessions will be disclosed to anybody under any circumstances. No supervisor, and only some consultants can give this total assurance. It is therefore essential to clarify *what* kind of information may be disclosed. (e.g. about clients or consultees), *how* it will be disclosed (e.g. written/verbal), and *to whom* (e.g. consultant's consultant, consultee's supervisor). The example which follows illustrates how lack of clarity about confidentiality can create difficulties.

> *Example:*
> a supervisee, with several years' post-qualification experience, asked his supervisor for help with his use of humour and joking in his work. He was later angry and dismayed to find adverse comment on this habit referred to explicitly in his evaluation report prepared for senior management. He and his supervisor obviously had very different understandings about the confidentiality status of his disclosure.

*Accountability* In statutory agencies where the consultant is not the supervisor, and cannot carry organisational accountability, the consultee needs to clarify with his supervisor, perhaps by including her in part of the contract negotiations, how agency accountability requirements can be maintained. One way is by regular reports from the consultee to the supervisor.

*The position of the clients* Clients who disclose personal information have a right to know of any limits to confidentiality. They should therefore be told of the existence of consultant or supervisor, as someone with whom their information will be shared in order to help their worker provide a more effective agency service. Most clients are pleased to know that the worker is getting this kind of help, but some may ask questions about it. In participant models there is direct contact and a relationship with the clients. In non-participant models clients sometimes develop a fascination with this 'ghost' person, and it is an interesting point whether some early meeting, probably informal, is a useful way of testing mutual client-consultant fantasies. Whatever approach is adopted, it is the consultee's responsibility to communicate about it with his clients.

*Recording* If a consultant wants some recorded information in advance of each session, it is necessary to clarify exactly what is wanted. For example, if some work is being tape-recorded the consultee may select and number those sections he would like the consultant to listen to (or view). This helps the consultant to prepare more effectively, and it is also a useful discipline for the consultee. (Incidentally, listening to, or viewing, tapes of your own work can be very informative and a good basis for do-it-yourself consultancy).

*Compatability* If signs of possible incompatability (whether of personality, theoretical framework or value-system) become apparent to the consultee at this contract stage, then, difficult as it may be, he should voice his misgivings rather than slide into an agreement he is not happy about, and which is unlikely to be productive.

## The consultee and the consultancy session

If all the preparatory work has been thoroughly done, the sessions themselves have every chance of being successful! There are, though, some additional skills to learn, both in immediate preparation for, and during, the actual sessions.

*Creating the space* Ideally, the consultee needs to allow a margin of time either side of the agreed time-boundaries of the session to facilitate punctuality, to arrive in a suitable state of mental preparation and motivation, and to try to avoid 'switching-off' in the last few minutes as the next commitment approaches.

*Preparing an agenda* The proactive consultee will come to the consultancy session with a clear agenda of items he wants to work at, in some order of priority, and with some thought out idea of the specific kind of help he wants from the consultant. If there are co-workers, then they can work out their agenda and approach between themselves in advance: if they cannot agree, that in itself may be an important agenda item. Agenda preparation is a way of ensuring the consultee's interests are paramount, although it may be agreed that the consultant includes her items also, as will happen in supervision.

*Communicating clearly* The consultee needs to communicate his concerns as accurately as possible. This is relatively straightforward with facts and content, but more difficult with expressive material. It is however important that emotion is communicated, and if there are confusion and irrational feelings inside the consultee, these need expression as important data for the consultant. Whatever the feeling, be it anger, despair, euphoria, frustration, elation, or hopelessness, it matters and is legitimate. No skilled consultant expects a wholly rational discussion with consultees who work with people in difficult and often distressing circumstances.

*Risk-taking* Consultancy sessions based on trust provide an opportunity for risk-taking in a secure environment. By risk-taking I mean disclosing 'mistakes', controversial material, or feelings of inadequacy or vulnerability, for example being honest about the strong feelings you may have about certain clients, officials or the agency, about problems in your work-relationship with a colleague, owning fear, love and hate, and so on. The consultant's response to an early personal disclosure will indicate whether trust is developing and an open approach can be used.

*Feedback to the consultant* The consultee cannot directly control the consultant's responses, but he has every right to try and influence them if they are unhelpful, irrelevant, upsetting, confusing or diverging from the agreement. To do this, the consultee may have to be direct or assertive to a higher status person or colleague. The feedback can either be immediate or made later during a periodic review of the consultancy. Negative feedback is not the only kind of feedback that a consultant needs (!): positive feedback about helpful responses, actions, comments or advice will enable her to do her job better, which can only benefit the consultee.

*Taking the role of consultee* This is a role to be learned like any other. It needs special attention when the normal work-role of the consultant is similar in status to that of the consultee, as in peer consultancy; when the consultee is very experienced not only as a practitioner but also as a consultant; and when two or more co-workers of different status become co-consultees. Being able to think and feel yourself into an appropriate role for a given context requires flexibility, and senior people becoming consultees need a humility that recognises they still have much to learn.

*Example:*
A student unit supervisor and a student he was supervising co-led a group and sought consultancy from an outsider. The supervisor might easily have paired with the consultant to focus on the student's work and development. This possibility was anticipated at the contract stage when

work was done on the roles to be taken. The consultancy was successful because the supervisor was able to make the role-change and focus on *his* needs as group-leader and co-worker. This was confirmed by a comment from the student that he felt 'freed' from the student supervisee role during the triadic consultancy sessions.

*Sticking to task* It is not enough to rely on the consultant to keep the work focused on task. The consultee needs to check his agenda periodically and to self-monitor during the session, being prepared when necessary to take the initiative of bringing discussion back to task if it has become anecdotal or diversionary.

## The consultee in different types of consultancy, and as supervisee

The above principles and guidelines for the consultee are based on the tutorial model, but they apply with some modifications to all other consultancy models, and to supervision. Group models will be discussed in Chapter 5, but some special features of *peer-pairs*, *participant consultancy* and *supervision* are now considered.

### *Peer-pairs*

This is the model in which the role of the consultee is most likely to get blurred, and the contract-making stage to be neglected. Colleagues who work together in the same staff-group, who have much informal and *ad hoc* contact, and who reciprocate the consultant-consultee roles in their peer pair, need to make a special effort to set up clear boundaries and role-delineation for their consultancy sessions. One of the real problems of this model is to be able to challenge and make demands of a colleague you know well. Special rituals like meeting in an unfamiliar room can help to mark the role-change and reduce collusion. A clear agreement, rather than 'can I use you if I need you?', will avoid the kind of situation when the consultee having made no effort to arrange any consultancy, comes along to the peer consultant near the end of the piece of work saying 'Things are in an awful mess, can you help?', putting the consultant in an almost impossible position.

### *Participant Consultancy*

In *live consultancy* without a screen, the role-relationship of consultee and consultant is more complex than in non-participant consultancy because the two are also co-workers in the sense that they are working together continually throughout the whole intervention process, albeit in very different roles. This gives the 'selection of consultant' and 'contract negotiation' phases a new significance and as Carpenter (1984) has shown, compatability testing, for example on theory, practice and value assumptions, needs to be as thoroughgoing as for any form of co-work. It is also essential to agree a series of ground-rules, for example how to introduce the method to the clients, and whether the consultee has to 'obey' the consultant.

Regarding the consultee role in the work sessions with clients, Kingston and Smith (1983) state that 'The particular skill required in working with a consultant is that of accepting advice on the spot, though it may not be congruent with the direction in which the therapist was already moving.' This method thus requires an additional consultee skill of being able, 'live', to listen simultaneously to messages from the family, yourself internally *and* the consultant, and to reconcile them in a way that takes the work forward positively. One way of dealing with overload is to take 'time out' for brief consultation. As co-worker, the consultant inevitably becomes part of the working process, and there may be times when the consultant-consultee pair need to seek non-participant consultancy, whether from a peer group or an individual consultant.

In *periodic on site* consultancy as described earlier, the consultee has to be prepared for active interventions by the consultant with 'his' clients (e.g. demonstrating play with a child). He is much less likely to feel undermined if there is a clear agreement with the consultant about the basis on which she may intervene. In all participant and observed models it is normal for the consultee to feel anxious and threatened by the prospect of direct scrutiny and live consultant interventions, but actual experience of the many positive aspects including active support and improved quality of work can make it much more acceptable and attractive.

## The Supervisee

As supervisee, the worker is in an involuntary relationship with his line-manager. Certain administrative functions and agency requirements *have* to take place within this role-relationship in which one person has delegated authority over the other. Regarding consultancy needs however, the supervisee has some choice and room for negotiation. The student or newly appointed worker must expect most, but by no means all, of his consultancy needs to be met within an individual and/or group supervision model, but the more experienced worker can seek consultancy from various sources, his supervisor being only one possibility. Whatever the career stage of the supervisee, contract negotiation with his supervisor is a basis for establishing rights, responsibilities and choices. Examples of the successful use of supervision contracts are given in a brief article, 'A working agreement', by a former team-leader, Christine North (1982).

The authority and power dimension in the supervisory relationship makes its impact, and the supervisee will need to test for trust and expectations. He has to make a judgement about whether, and when to disclose 'weakness', shortcomings and difficulties. Some supervisors regard self-disclosure as a strength in a supervisee and will evaluate it positively (unless it is excessive or quite inappropriate). Others may evaluate disclosure of shortcomings negatively, perhaps 'caseworking' or 'theraping' the supervisee in the process. The supervisee needs to 'know thy supervisor' and manage his self-presentation and self-disclosure accordingly. At best, supervision based on a mutually trusting relationship, can offer high quality consultancy. At worst, all kinds of problems and games-playing can develop. In 'Games Supervisees Play' Kadushin (1969) lists reasons why supervisees may need to defend against possible losses, and so try to control the situation to their own advantage by games-playing.

The reasons are: anxiety about the expectation of change; threat to independence and autonomy; threat to sense of adequacy; threat to self and felt inadequacies; reactivation of parent–child and sibling–sibling relationships; and supervisor's access to important rewards and penalties. Most of these have already been touched on, but not 'reactivation of parent–child and sibling–sibling relationships'. A degree of quasi-sibling rivalry and competitiveness is almost inevitable among peers in a staff-group. One good way to deal with this is to bring it out into the open in the group, but an outside consultant may be needed to facilitiate this process (see Chapter 5).

Kadushin identifies the following 'supervisee games':

(1) *Manipulating demand levels*:
    'Two against the agency' in which the supervisee pushes the professional valency against the bureaucratic, getting the supervisor to collude;
(2) *Redefining the relationship*:
    as worker–client, friend–friend, or peer–peer;
(3) *Reducing power disparity* or 'putting the supervisor down':
    'if you knew Dostoevsky as I know Dostoevsky';
    'so what do *you* know about it', re some topic the supervisor knows little about;

(4) *Controlling the situation*:
   'I did it like you told me' (and it failed!)
   'Heading them off at the pass' (early admission of many mistakes);
   providing topics which the supervisor likes talking about, thus taking the heat off the supervisee.

*Supervisors* also play games (Hawthorne 1979) because they sometimes feel threatened, uncertain about their authority, want to be liked, and so on. Their games include:

(1) '*I wonder why you really said that*' – converting awkward questions into psychological resistance;
(2) *Games of abdication*:
   'They won't let me', 'poor me', 'I'm really one of you';
(3) *Games of power*:
   'Remember who's boss', 'I'll tell on you', 'Mother knows best', 'I'm only trying to help you'.

Whilst these kinds of games are quite amusing caricatures to reflect on, they are mostly unproductive, if not destructive, and an obstacle to effective supervisory consultancy. There are some things a supervisee can do to reduce the games-playing. As a start, he needs to acknowledge that his supervisor is a person as well as a role, that she has a difficult job with competing loyalties, that she too can experience anxiety and threat, and that she is likely to respond warmly to positive feedback about things she does well. More specifically, the supervisee can do one or more of the following: try to stop his own games-playing (i.e. refuse to play); confront his supervisor with what is happening in their interactions; share openly his awareness of obstacles to effective supervision; or present his own professional needs for consultancy and negotiate agreement about which may best be met by supervision, and which by other forms of consultancy and training.

**Summary**

The common thread running through this chapter is that there is much that the proactive worker himself can do to try and obtain the kind of consultation and supervision that he needs, appropriate to his own career-stage. We have indicated ways in which a consultee's behaviour in the consultation process may be influenced by his learning and work-styles, as well as by the consultancy context and the consultant herself. The concept of *consultee-style* emerges as a useful term to describe the behaviours and attitudes which typify a particular worker in the consultee role. As with work-style, consultee-style can be developed creatively to extend the individual's repertoire to include a wider range of consultee roles and contexts, such as participant, peer and group methods.

# 3 The Consultant

We now turn to the consultant and her skills. The last chapter is a reminder that all consultants will have past (and frequently present) experiences of the consultee role 'inside them', influencing expectations of how they should behave as consultant, and enabling them to empathise with the consultee(s) whom they are trying to help. Many of the qualities suggested for the consultee apply to the consultant also, but with the difference that the consultant's concern is primarily for the consultee and his clients whereas the consultee is there to meet his own needs, albeit in order to provide a better service for his clients.

Four main sources of consultancy were identified in Chapter 1: supervisor, peer, agency specialist and outsider. To these was added a fifth, the team (a combination of supervisor and peers, see Chapters 5 and 6). Each of these sources carries a different kind of role-relationship with the consultee, and each has its advantages and disadvantages. These differences and their implications for the consultant's self-management and skills will be discussed later in this chapter. We shall first discuss the basic stance, skills, techniques, pitfalls and dilemmas of the 'non-participant' and 'observing' consultant. Participant consultancy, to which much of this basic material also applies with suitable modifications, is considered later, as are the special features of consultancy in methods of work with clients in groups. The chapter concludes with a brief reference to ways of learning the skills of consultancy.

## The stance of the consultant

I can do no better, following Kaslow (1977), than quote from *The Prophet* (Gibran 1975), a suitable piece to be read by consultants at regular intervals!

> Then said a teacher, speak to us of Teaching.
> And he said:
> No man can reveal to you aught but that which already lies half asleep in the dawning of your knowledge.
> The teacher who walks in the shadow of the temple, among his followers, gives not of his wisdom but rather of his faith and his lovingness.
> If he is indeed wise, he does not bid you enter the house of his wisdom, but rather leads you to the threshold of your own mind.
> . . . For the vision of one man lends not its wings to another man.

Downes and Hall (1977) put it another way at the end of their useful article about consultation within social work, 'Such "knowing idiocy" as the consultant enjoys frees the social worker to make use of his own sure knowledge and so gives time for his wits to return and confusion lessen.' This philosophical stance of facilitated self-learning is not only likely to be an effective approach, but it should also help the neophyte or would-be consultant to appreciate that the main virtue is not to be the 'super-expert', but to have enough skill, understanding and relevant knowledge to enable the other person(s) to work out their own solutions and ways of moving forward. If, as practitioner, the consultant works (or worked) with clients in this way, then no major adaptation will be needed.

## The contact stage

A prospective consultancy arrangement begins at the point at which a potential consultant is approached, either by a prospective consultee or by some third party such as an agency manager. The way in which the first approach is made, and who makes it, can be very revealing of motivations (for consultancy, and for this particular consultant), expectations and possible hidden agendas. The consultant needs therefore to be both responsive and cautious in her first reaction, particularly if the approach is by a third party or by one member of a co-working pair or group when there is some uncertainty about the attitudes and wishes of absent colleague(s). The dilemma is how to obtain more information without probing and raising too many obstacles. If it is a new contact for the potential consultee the first response of the consultant will also be a kind of trailer of the way she works. It is usually necessary for the consultant to ask preliminary questions about: purpose; who the consultee(s) will be; and practical matters such as timing, frequency and fee (if relevant). Clear exchange of information and expectations at the pre-contract stage can save time and resources.

*Example:*
A Social Services Department sought consultancy from a University lecturer some 80 miles away. The telephone request for consultancy on the management of staff stress turned out in subsequent face-to-face discussion to be a request for consultancy on workload management, a different kind of skill which the potential consultant did not have. This could have been clarified over the telephone.

Circumstances, and therefore the response, will vary enormously, from the apprehensive and perhaps ambivalent consultee approaching a high status outside consultant for the first time, to an experienced worker asking a long-standing colleague for a peer–pair, or live–consultancy arrangement. Whatever the circumstances, there are important feelings and technical issues to be recognised and worked out in the initial transaction. One issue is how to differentiate the potential consultant role (pre-contract) from the actual consultant role (post-contract). For example, when responding to an enquiry from a potential consultee I have to check myself sometimes from behaving as though I was already in a consultancy role-relationship with him.

It can also happen that the first move is made by the consultant herself when, for whatever reason, she tries to initiate a consultancy service. We are not primarily concerned here with this type of consultant-initiated consultancy except when we come to consider supervision consultancy, but it is worth noting that American studies cited by Kadushin (1977, Chapter 4) confirm that such approaches often run into serious difficulties.

**The contract stage**
Assuming both parties are satisfied that it is worth proceeding, the next step is to arrange a meeting to discuss the contract (or 'agreement'). The consultant would normally want to meet all the consultees and in some circumstances it may be desirable to include the consultee's supervisor, at least for part of the time. The need for all consultees to be present is to ensure that all are party to the contract, and the presence of the supervisor might be necessary when the three-way relationship is likely to be delicate, and/or to clarify issues about accountability and resources. The consultee may not wish his supervisor to be present, but in some circumstances (e.g. when the supervisor's support is essential), the consultant may deem it politic to have a personal meeting with her (with the consultee's consent) whether or not it is separate from the main contract session.

The contract-making meeting has important process and task elements. The process element is the 'joining' of consultant and consultee(s), in that initial engagement, which can set the foundations for a good working relationship. The usual joining techniques apply, including warmth, friendliness, initial social exchanges, individual contact with each participant, and the provision of a welcoming physical environment (if this meeting is on consultee territory, then the consultant may pick up much useful information from the way she is received). The consultant needs to be sensitive to the feelings being expressed, or revealed, by the consultee(s), and to facilitate the articulation of any suppressed feelings or information which is likely to be relevant to the viability of the contract and the consultancy.

> *Example*:
> Two social work colleagues, a man and a woman, showed very excitable behaviour at the contract-meeting and in the first few consultancy sessions. It only transpired later that they had just started living together, not in itself necessarily relevant information, but in this case it was very obviously influencing their co-working and the consultancy sessions. The consultant had decided earlier not to comment on her observation of their behaviour, but later wondered if the risk should have been taken.

The *task* components of the contract were discussed in the previous chapter and will not be repeated here. There are however several questions of particular relevance to the consultant at this stage:

– Is the purpose clear, and what are the consultee(s)' expectations of the consultant role and what consultancy may achieve?
– Who comprises the consultee system?
– What role-relationship, if any, will the consultant have with: the consultee's supervisor; his clients; other relevant people (e.g. team-members, training officers, volunteers)?
– What is the general attitude of the consultee? Are there any indications that he may feel coerced into attending? How anxious is he? Is he clear about what he wants? Is he relatively new to consultancy and experiencing it as quite threatening? Is he well motivated to work?
– Are any methods going to be used which will make extra demands on the consultee (e.g. all forms of participant consultancy, observation, use of tapes, use of experiential techniques in consultancy sessions)? If so, these methods need full discussion and an agreement that their use is acceptable to all participants.
– Most importantly, if the contract-meeting reveals agency or consultee terms which are unacceptable to the consultant, or if there is a real likelihood of incompatability (whether of personality, values or theoretical approach), the consultant should decline the contract giving her reasons. One consultancy skill is to model the ability to say 'no' in an acceptable way when the occasion requires it.

## Preparation for the consultancy sessions

The interval between the agreement of a contract and the first consultancy session is the period of preparation. During this time there is an opportunity for the consultant to inform herself about the work-context of the consultee(s). This is most necessary for the outside consultant who may know little about the agency, its responsibilities, organisation and procedures. Often the consultees can supply relevant general documentation as well as specific reports or records relevant to the consultancy work. How much of this advance 'information' preparation should be done is a point of some disagreement among consultants. Those with a strong problem-solving orientation would say it is essential background, whereas those with a process orientation argue that it is too pre-emptive and controlling of the consultee, and that the consultant should arrive at the first session without preconceived solutions, wide open to whatever the consultee brings.

The consultant who has no strong bias to task or process will be influenced in her preparation by the contract agreement about purpose and methods. Whilst there is legitimate controversy about the extent of content preparation, it is desirable that all consultants do some 'internal' preparatory work, by reflecting on their own feelings, attitudes, hopes, prejudices and hidden agendas, as the first session approaches. In some instances of particularly complex or daunting consultancy assignments, the consultant may seek consultancy help herself in preparing for the task.

*Example*:
A consultant was engaged by the staff of a psychiatric unit to help them work at issues of interprofessional communication and collaboration in the hospital. The consultees were a group of nearly twenty staff from several disciplines, and with many agendas. The consultant (with the full knowledge of the consultees) benefited both in preparation and during the consultancy period from some consultancy sessions of her own with a 'consultant's consultant'.

Preparation once consultancy has begun is also essential, both in familiarising yourself with any advance information, for example records, tapes, and in preparing mentally for each session by, for instance, allocating time corridors around sessions as suggested for consultees. Little is known about the recording habits of consultants, but it is useful to keep brief records of consultancy meetings which can be referred to in preparation for subsequent meetings, and in review and evaluation.

**Consultancy skills**
As in social work practice, a blend of process and task skills is

required, with the emphasis likely to vary according to the consultant's style and theoretical position as well as the consultee's preoccupations and the nature of the consultancy task. Kadushin (1977) produced some interesting evidence from American research studies which showed that whilst consultants and consultees rated both process and task skills as important, the consultees tended to emphasise problem-solving as the first priority more than the consultants did. My view is that a blend of the two is essential for a desired outcome in which the consultee both feels better in himself *and* works more effectively. The following repertoire of consultancy skills, which includes a balance of process and task elements, is not very different from those needed by the practitioner in his work with clients.

*Relationship skills* The establishment of good working relationship, renewed at the joining stage of each session, is a *sine qua non* of effective consultancy. The Truax and Carkhuff (1967) qualities of *empathy, genuineness* and *non-possessive warmth* are especially important early on in a session during the 'exposition phase' when the consultee is trying, perhaps anxiously, to communicate both information and feelings about the issues which concern him. His whole self-presentation, mood and gestures can be as significant as the content. The consultant needs to *listen, observe* and *encourage* in a culture of *acceptance, support* and *positive reinforcement*. New consultees may also need help from the consultant with learning how to take the role appropriately and use it to best advantage.

*Elaboration skills* As the consultee outlines the issue, problem or need, the consultant can facilitate the process by again *listening* very carefully and then helping the consultee to *elaborate, clarify* and *focus*. This may include *partialising the problem* to make it more manageable, and *establishing priorities*. The consultancy skill lies in enabling the consultee to do this in his own language and framework, avoiding the temptation to redefine the material in the consultant's own terms and conceptual framework.

*Problem-solving facilitation skills* In any one consultancy session it is useful to aim at completing the stage of exposition and clarification of the problem by the mid-point or earlier, allowing enough time to work at possible resolutions and ways of moving forward. The consultee may get bogged down in 'problem-talking' and description, and need some help in making this shift in focus.

The skill of the consultant lies not in solving the problem herself, but in facilitating a process which enables the consultee to generate ideas, consider their relative merits, and move towards possible plans for future action. The consultee's ideas are likely to be the most fruitful as he knows the client context best, but there is a place for the consultant to make suggestions and offer advice, particularly when the consultee is inexperienced, stuck or both. Consultees do get frustrated by purist consultants who just sit there, nod and look wise! Before the end of the session the consultee and the consultant together need to have developed some ideas which will contribute to the consultee's next stage of work with his client(s). Any proposed course of action generated in a consultancy session is best left open-ended and unfinished, so the consultee can think further and make his own decisions later.

*Skills of challenging, confronting and offering feedback* Shulman (1982), following Schwartz (1971), refers to 'skills in making a demand for work'. He is writing about supervision skills where the authority to make such a demand is clear. In non-supervisory consultancy the authority of the consultant to challenge and make demands is less clear, resting as it does on a professional agreement to work together, and an implicit or explicit mandate permitting the consultant (and indeed the consultee!) to confront (in the non-pejorative, non-aggressive sense) if the need arises. Evasive, negative or games-playing behaviour will always have an explanation, for example coercion, anxiety, exhaustion, but for that to emerge and be discussed some *direct feedback* is sometimes both necessary and helpful. Smith (1980) has shown that a combination of support and confrontation is particularly effective in producing change. The consultant is also modelling 'straight-talking' in a way which may be useful to the consultee in his work with clients.

Another dimension of this skill is *confrontation* of difficult topics and obstacles to progress. This includes possible taboo areas (e.g. sexual feelings about clients, dislike of a colleague, and issues of authority and dependence) which frequently distort the consultancy work-relationship, and not only when it forms part of supervision.

*Skills in sharing own feelings* There is some evidence, (Shulman 1978; Chelune 1979) that self-disclosure skills play an important part in the helping process. The essence of the skills is behaving as the person you are but within the professional role. This includes expressing feelings, and owning vulnerability and the making of mistakes when these occur. This integration of the personal and the professional also has modelling value.

*Skills in pacing* The consultant has a special responsibility to be aware of time-boundaries and the pacing of a session, taking into account the consultee's needs and preoccupations. A mental picture of a flexible sequence of stages may help, i.e. joining, agenda setting, problem identification and clarification, generation of possible solutions, and discussion of tentative plans for moving forward, review and termination.

*Ending skills* The ending of a session should not be too rushed, allowing time for recapping if needed, but also enabling the consultee to leave the session feeling it has been of some value, with some new perceptions and ideas generated, and confidence to face the challenges to come.

*Review and evaluation* Evaluation applies both to the work done by the consultee with his clients (an important aspect of practice for which consultancy may be sought, but outside the scope of this book), and to the consultancy process itself. With regard to the latter, the consultant needs to check with the consultees at intervals whether they are experiencing the sessions and her interventions as useful, and how they might be improved. If done too frequently this probably indicates consultant insecurity and reassurance-seeking, and is not helpful to the consultee. Part of the final session, or a special meeting, needs to be set aside to review the consultancy work overall. 'Yes/No' questions like 'has it been useful?' may not produce informative or accurate replies. More specific questions, perhaps asking for detailed comment on both the useful and less useful aspects, can provide a more authentic response. Some find it easier to criticise on paper. In her management of review and evaluation the consultant needs to be aware that she is again modelling an approach which may be followed by the consultee.

*Awareness of the 'mirroring' effect of the 'reflection process'*
Searles (1955) observed that 'the processes at work currently in the *relationship between client and worker* are often reflected in the *relationship between worker and supervisor*'. Mattinson (1975) has discussed this phenomenon using material from workshops for supervisors. She uses a psycho-dynamic conceptual framework, for example transference and counter-transference, which will be more familiar and more acceptable to some readers than others, but there is little doubt that the phenomenon of mirroring that she describes frequently occurs and influences the consultancy transaction. There cannot be many consultants who have not been bewildered by what they are made to feel sometimes by the consultee's presentation of himself and his material. An example of this is when the client transfers his feelings of helplessness and impotence to his social worker, who then unknowingly transfers them to his supervisor.

She in turn may feel inadequate, and seek consultation from her supervisor . . . This 'mirroring' also goes in the other direction, so that if, for example, the consultant communicates 'therapeutic optimism' to the consultee, he in turn may enable his clients to feel more hopeful. When done consciously, this is a form of behaviour modelling.

The consultant needs to be sensitive to mirroring effects, so that firstly she does not get unhelpfully caught up in the worker-client dynamic which has been imported into the consultancy relationship, and secondly so she can help the worker to understand what he is 'carrying for the client', and use that understanding to free him and the client to work together more productively. *Note*: the client may be a group not an individual, as for example in residential work, when there is sometimes an interactive mirroring between the staff and the residents' group.

**Consultancy techniques**
In addition to the general skills just outlined, consultants (in non-participant and observed models of consultancy) can use various techniques to increase the consultee's learning:
*Talking/discussion* Much consultancy relies exclusively on talking, but there are wide variations in how the talking is structured ranging from 'free association' at one extreme to meticulously planned and organised dialogue at the other. The model suggested here blends clarity of boundaries, focus and task with flexibility and a sensitive response to feelings, mood and relationship.
*Role-play* can be a very effective medium for consultancy work and it can be used in two principal ways. The first is *retrospective*, with the re-enactment of a problematic episode or critical incident. The consultee, by taking the client role and experiencing someone else in his own role (role-reversal), and then perhaps trying a new approach to the same incident in his own role, can re-experience what happened and gain new understanding.

The other, *prospective* use of role-play is for *rehearsal* of an approach to be taken at the next stage, the consultancy session providing a relatively secure environment to risk trying something new and difficult.

*Example*:
A consultee is having great difficulty in working with a family because the alcoholic father is always drunk at the arranged family sessions. In consultancy he is helped to see that he is colluding with the family in allowing this behaviour to block any possibility of useful work. Role-play

is used to practice various techniques, for example confrontation, or a strategic intervention, which the consultee might use to try and unblock the impasse.

Consultancy models which involve several consultees together, e.g. group supervision, offer much more scope for role-play, but role-reversal and related techniques can be effective in a one-to-one context.

*Sculpting* is now quite a familiar technique in training and in some forms of practice, such as family therapy. It can also be used to good advantage in consultancy work when the consultee is enabled to use this creative technique which relies principally on visual and kinaesthetic (i.e. feelings) rather than verbal communication, to re-enact the pair, family or group system of relatedness, and the role of the worker. It can also be used in consultancy training as a way of understanding the dynamics of the consultant-consultee(s) relationship.

*Selective use of video and audio tapes* The essence of these recordings is what the *worker himself* learns from seeing and/or hearing himself in action. The skill of the consultant lies not in providing a brilliant analysis of what happened, or in pointing out all the errors of the consultee, but rather in gently facilitating the worker's own learning and insights through discussion of what they have both observed/listened to. The consultant may also be able to help the 'reluctant taper' to gain the confidence to try it, and to rehearse ways of introducing its possible use to the client. My experience is that the worker's own attitude to taping is usually transmitted to the clients, and has a major influence on their response.

*Brainstorming* This familiar technique can be useful in the early or middle stages of a problem-solving consultancy session, as a means of generating a large range of ideas quickly.

**Consultancy pitfalls and dilemmas**

*Being too passive or too directive* Most consultees do not want their consultant to be either the silent contemplator or the rapid problem-solver. A creative skill of the facilitator role is judging when to offer and when to withhold direction and suggestions.

*'Taking over' or 'practice by proxy'* A seductive trap for the consultant, particularly if she no longer practises herself, is to work with the clients by proxy, using the consultee as an agent to carry out her own approach vicariously.

*Example*:
In the middle of a consultancy session ideas are being generated about what a residential worker should do when one child in a group watching TV refuses to go to bed at the appointed time. The consultant suggests that he could ask the other children *their* views. The consultee refers to this as 'a good idea', adopting it uncritically, and the consultant then checks herself, realising that she is reinforcing dependency and getting close to 'taking over'.

Participant consultants are susceptible to this danger in a different way because they are in face-to-face contact with clients with the opportunity to control consultee *and* clients.

*Consultants are human too* Consultees are often encouraged to share vulnerability and personal anxieties with their consultant. This is made more difficult, and more unlikely, if the consultant (and even more so the supervisor) models non-disclosing, non-anxious behaviour. Apart from the inequity, this may reinforce the consultee's feelings of inadequacy and incompetence.

*Splitting off the supervisor* For non-supervisor consultants there can be a temptation to create, or reinforce, splits between worker and supervisor, either by directly undermining the latter's position, authority and competence, or more subtly by identifying with a consultee's organisational role. This can only be destructive long-term, and consultees need help in reconciling the range of interests which impinge on their work.

## The consultant role in participant consultancy

The common feature of all participant models is the direct involvement which the consultant has with the clients. This makes it essential that the respective roles of consultant and consultee are clear to all concerned, including the clients. In *joint work* this clarity is especially necessary because many different co-working roles are possible, for example the consultant taking the secondary or the primary role. Whatever pattern is agreed, the consultant-consultee relationship 'sub-system' is a reality that cannot be discounted in the shared working. In *live-consultancy* the precise role and authority of the consultant needs to be known, and in particular whether the role is truly consultant, that is leaving the consultee free to accept or reject consultant suggestions, or supervisory, that is able to give instructions to be obeyed. Another important point is whether the consultant can make direct communications with the clients.

*Periodic on-site consultancy* calls for rather different consultancy skills, because although the consultant intervenes directly with worker and client, on site, for much of the time she is absent. The skill lies therefore in knowing (1) when to be around at all, (2) when you are around, when to actually intervene with staff or clients or both, and (3) how to intervene in ways which enhance rather than diminish worker confidence, scrupulously avoiding pressures to appear to the clients as a worker they would prefer to have.

All types of participant consultancy include additional sessions in which consultant and consultee(s) meet alone to do the planning, review and evaluation work. The shared work experience enriches these sessions in many ways; the problem for the consultant being how to become sufficiently disengaged from the shared work context to facilitate the consultee's own learning and development.

## Consultancy for social work with clients in groups

This section refers to consultancy for work with clients in family groups, community groups, formed groups, peer groups and living groups in residential settings. References have been given (Chapter 1) to the specialist literature for these different contexts, but there are a few general points which arise from the increased complexity of work with groups.

The meaning of *client-centred consultation* in work with groups depends on the extent to which 'the client' is regarded as the group-as-a-whole (as in group system-focused models of practice) or as each individual group member (as in models which use individually focused work in a group context). This issue needs discussing and clarifying at the contract stage, and reflecting upon periodically during consultancy sessions to see the kind of focus that both consultant and consultees are *actually* using in their work together, and how this relates to the focus being used by the consultee in his practice.

*Worker-centred consultation* also takes on a whole new dimension when, as often happens in work with groups, there are two or more co-workers. This creates a 'worker-system' so the consultancy focus may be either on the individual workers, or on the working pair/group and their co-working relationship, or both. A reasonable assumption is that in most client and most worker groups there will be some important issues which are primarily individual and others which stem from the interactional group processes. To exclude either is to over-simplify.

The co-working relationship (see Galinsky and Schopler 1980) will sometimes be the agreed primary focus of consultancy because in co-led groups the quality of the worker partnership can be a major determinant of the success or failure of the group. As in marriages and families, the emotional involvement of the consultees with each other sets limits to how far they can resolve interpersonal work problems unaided. The consultant has a vital role to play in opening up communication between the workers on the more difficult issues, clarifying their role-relationship, and enabling them to use their individual and combined talents productively. Helping them to share with each other what they feel about working together and about each other's style and contribution in the group can release energy previously locked up in co-working tension, which is then available for the clients' benefit.

*Example*:
Two social workers who had not worked together before undertook the ambitious task of co-leading a multiple-family group, that is three or four complete families in one group. What emerged in consultancy was a power-struggle for dominance in the working pair. The consultant explored this with them and discovered that each of them had always taken the dominant role in previous pairings with other colleagues. This insight brought tremendous relief, and with consultant help they were able to work out a mutually acceptable way of sharing the leadership in future sessions, thus freeing themselves to concentrate on member needs rather than their own battle.

Consultancy help with co-working pairs ideally starts at the pre-group stage when the couple or trio are helped to share expectations and anxieties about the group itself and their own working relationship.

*Example*:
In preparation for a group for bereaved people, it transpired at a pre-group consultancy session that neither partner had shared with the other his own personal experience and feelings about death, grief and mourning. This was essential pre-group work, as is sharing about personal family perspectives when doing conjoint family work.

*Mediating conflict. The community work consultant* may find herself in the role of 'conflict mediator' between groups, and in particular between community workers and their own employers. Briscoe (1977) suggests the internal consultant may be in a better position than the external consultant to assist with community worker-employer conflicts because of her established credibility in a recognised role within the organisation. She could on the other hand find neutrality a more difficult position to maintain as an agency employee with a possible vested interest, than she would as a recognised independent consultant. In either model, the initial contract needs to be carefully drawn up so everyone knows whether the consultee is the community worker, management, or both (a form of inter-group consultancy).

**The external consultant**
The suggestion made earlier that the initial reaction to a consultancy request be 'responsive but cautious' applies particularly to the external consultant who will often be ignorant about the context of the request. The caution is to ensure that motivations are reasonably explicit, and that the conditions offered are acceptable. When a fee is paid, and a contractual obligation established, there is sometimes greater role and function clarity than when informal arrangements evolve in what may be a confused and confusing manner. The external consultant's source of authority is her professional expertise, and her potency depends as much on the consultee's validation of her role, as on her actual competence. The potency can be frustrated, or even sabotaged, when there is political or personal in-fighting in the background to the consultancy. In such circumstances, the external consultant needs to maintain an independent stance when subjected to pressures to align with one faction against another. This problem may be avoided if (1) wherever the initial approach comes from, the relevant consultees are clearly identified and included in the contract negotiations, and (2) 'significant others' who may be immediately affected by the consultancy arrangements are included in some part of the negotiations and agreement. This refers particularly to consultees' colleagues and supervisors. The latter will need to be satisfied that accountability for work done by consultees is linked into the normal supervisory channels.

Once the consultancy sessions are under way the skills are essentially those already described. The external consultant, at least initially, may be attributed with almost miraculous skills, an expectation which she will not be able to live up to(!) and which will detract from the consultee being helped to discover and use his own skills and abilities. The message here is to be realistic right from the beginning about what you can and cannot offer.

**The internal consultant**
Agency-appointed 'official' internal consultants often have to work very hard to establish their credibility with both potential consultees, and supervisors. There is often confusion about the nature of their role and authority as they move between

management and practice, and between a general development function and offering a specific consultancy service to staff. Whilst many line-managers and supervisors welcome this use of specialist help for their staff, others may be ambivalent about what they view as an intrusion into their domain. One of the main skills of this type of consultant is to be able to operate across a complex of individual, team and area boundaries, establishing good communication networks and access, ensuring that accountability is always clear, and that the respective roles of specialist consultant and staff-supervisor are always defined and agreed.

The 'unofficial' internal consultant who gets approached by colleagues because of her acknowledged expertise and specialist interests, for example in behaviour modification or compulsory psychiatric admissions, can probably fit in a bit of consultancy help in addition to her personal workload, but anything beyond that needs to be negotiated with her supervisor for formal recognition. This then shifts the role into something more official with organisational implications, unless two teams or establishments agree to use each other's staff in this way on a *quid pro quo* basis. There are some 'career grade' or 'senior practitioner' posts with job specifications which include this type of cross-team consultancy work.

**The peer consultant**

This model depends on reciprocity between two or more workers who recognise one another as professional peers (whether or not their formal roles are similar), and who are motivated to help one another. Each worker will take consultant and consultee roles at different times and therefore needs the basic skills of each role. The additional factor in this model (and in peer groups) is the ability to differentiate the two roles clearly when working in each with the same colleagues. For example, when worker A is consultee, worker B's task as consultant is to concentrate solely on A's needs and interests, avoiding the temptation to follow interesting hares, anecdotes and other agendas which are especially likely to be around if the peer-pair are team-colleagues. Unhelpful competitiveness is another danger, and if it arises it is best dealt with by open discussion and agreed strategies for overcoming it in the mutual interest.

Most peer-consultants find it relatively easy to offer support to their consultee colleagues, but find it much more difficult to make demands, and if necessary to confront. There is no easy way round this except to note that in close secure working-relationships straight-talking is likely to be more appreciated. Blake and Mouton (1976) quote some research which suggests that the narrower the gap between the status of helper and helped, the more effective may be the changes that result. This indicates the considerable potential of peer consultancy, especially if collusion can be avoided.

*Supervisor consultancy skills*
The basic consultancy skills of the supervisor offering consultancy to her own staff as part of her supervisory function, are the same as those outlined throughout this chapter. However, additional skills and responsibilities derive from her managerial and supervisory roles. These roles give her certain authority and power over her supervisees, which, *inter alia*, enable her to make more demands of them during supervision-consultation, and to have more influence over their subsequent activities and decisions. The skill lies firstly in managing this legitimised power so that the supervisee's own skills and personal resources are enhanced, rather than crushed, and secondly in overcoming supervisee anxieties that an honest open approach will result in adverse evaluation.

Those supervisors who are likely to function effectively as consultants with their supervisees are those who:
– stay in role, and manage their authority and power in a professional way;
– recognise their own strengths and limitations;
– model the use of appropriate self-disclosure, and acknowledge personal vulnerability;
– talk quite explicitly with their staff, individually and as a group, about their supervision, consultancy and training needs;
– are secure enough to know what forms of help their supervisees can best find elsewhere, and support them in getting it;
– get good quality supervisory and consultancy support themselves;
– cope with the projections of feelings and frustration which their authority role will almost inevitably attract from supervisees;
– avoid as far as possible 'the games supervisors play' (Hawthorne 1979) and help supervisees to reduce their games-playing (see Chapter 2).

For a detailed account of supervisor skills see Shulman (1982).

## Learning the skills of consultancy
It is interesting to observe that whereas there are numerous courses and workshops on management, there are relatively few on consultancy. The prospective consultant, whether supervisor or

not, often finds herself having to learn about consultancy through experience, trial and error, with little to guide her. A few suggestions can be made:

(1) There are now some useful books, albeit North American and expensive, which give detailed attention to the *practice-skills* as well as the theory of consultancy (e.g. Kadushin 1977, Shulman 1982, Gallessich 1982).

(2) There are several other writers who consider consultancy style. Heron (1975), working in the human relations field, has developed six dimensions of facilitator style, for example confronting–non-confronting, structured-unstructured. Lippitt and Lippitt (1977), drawing on organisational studies, outline a continuum of consultancy roles and helping functions ranging from the more directive (e.g. advocate), to the more non-directive (e.g. process specialist). Hawkins (1982) suggests ways in which, through a content and process analysis of tape-recorded supervisory sessions, a supervisor can map her own style, providing an insight into the content, movement and focus of her supervision.

(3) Consultants, especially beginners, need consultancy themselves. The consultant's consultant can be a useful role-model, but more important is the explicit contribution the experienced consultant can make in facilitating trainee consultant skills using a similar range of skills to those described here.

(4) Courses and workshops on consultancy, in which consultancy skills and issues can be role-played, discussed and rehearsed in the supportive context of a peer-group, are an excellent way of learning.

# 4 The Student Stage

For many social workers their first experience of professional supervision occurs during practice placements on a training course. This is often an intensive experience which establishes attitudes and approaches to consultation, supervision and professional development which will influence the social worker for many years in his future career. (When experienced practitioners become supervisors themselves, they often draw heavily on the internalised role-model of the supervision they experienced as a student. My own training was twenty years ago, yet I can recall vividly the supervisory experiences of my two assessed placements.) It is most important, therefore, to identify some of the key elements and processes in the student practice training experience if these are to provide the newly qualified worker with a positive, creative orientation to consultancy and supervision in his future career.

There are several texts (e.g. Young 1967, Pettes 1979, Danbury 1979) which discuss student supervision quite comprehensively, although they are all written primarily for 'supervisors' (to be referred to hereafter as practice-teachers) and give little explicit attention to the student perspective. This chapter, whilst of necessity having to be very selective in content, will follow the general theme and philosophy of this text, giving particular attention to the student role and perspective, alongside that of the practice-teacher and not forgetting the rather uncertain role of the tutor. My selection of content has been influenced in part by a recent research study (Syson 1981) which examined in detail what actually happened on a sample of forty-one placements, undertaken by thirty-eight students from eight randomly selected CQSW courses. This report makes salutory reading and its conclusions, although drawn from a small sample of courses, are important for all students, practice-teachers, course tutors and agency managers. What it reveals is not only the wide variation in patterns and practices, but also the uneven quality of the practice placement experiences, and the many areas in which improvement is needed. Syson's findings confirm that careful, thorough and explicit preparation by all parties involved, prior to the placement, is a *sine qua non* for a 'successful' outcome, and this preparation stage will be given particular attention in what follows. Her study also confirmed that student learning and assessment was still based almost entirely on 'invisible' practice, and that links between practice and theoretical concepts taught on the course were tenuous or non-existent. These two areas will also be discussed.

What follows makes two working assumptions. The first is that placements form part of a full-time CQSW course (some of the material is also relevant to CSS training, but the CSS student's role as employee – and often a very experienced worker – does make for important differences). The second is that although the majority of courses have two or more assessed placements we shall, for convenience, refer to 'the placement', the emphasis assuming a final placement context.

### The student placement context

As background to what follows, we shall note briefly the special features which distinguish a student practice placement context, and its supervision, from that of an employee.

*Aims of the placement* These include services to clients, the acquisition of knowledge and skills, the professional development of the student, and assessment of practice competence. Whilst service to clients should never be compromised, the weighting of these various aims is not the same for students as it is for staff supervisees, because training requirements necessarily carry a high priority.

*Supervision and consultancy* Most consultancy which a student experiences will inevitably be as supervisee from his practice-teacher, but some opportunities for non-assessed practice and/or for consultation from other workers can provide useful if limited experience of consultancy outside of supervision.

*Time-limited supervision* Student placements are always time-limited, and often last only a few months. This introduces a time-span comparable to non-supervisory consultancy as distinct from the potentially indefinite time-span of staff supervision.

*Role-relationship with practice-teacher* The student role is quite complex because the student is a member of the 'host' agency operationally, but is not an employee. His practice-teacher has supervisory authority stemming from her delegated functions as teacher and assessor, but she is not his line-manager. She and the student both carry dual accountability to the agency and the training course.

*Supervision agenda* Whereas qualified staff and their supervisors need to be very selective about supervision agendas, the smaller workload and the training emphasis of the student mean all his work is part of the potential agenda, at least initially.

*'Novice' factor* Many students are inexperienced in social work, and this creates an appropriate dependency on the practice-teacher, but even so, there is considerable scope for adopting a proactive approach to supervision.

*The theory link* Students are expected to 'apply theory to practice' more consciously than are qualified staff. (This is a problematic area we shall return to near the end of the chapter.)

## General preparation for placement and supervision

General preparation for placement needs to begin when a student *starts* his training course (even if the first practice placement is as much as six months or more ahead). An excellent way to start a course is to set aside a period of time, say one week, which is devoted to a *self-positioning* programme. This term is used to describe a planned process (see Payne 1980 for a detailed account), in which an individual is helped to assemble and make conscious his 'baseline' of life experience, values, learning experiences, study skills, knowledge, social work practice, and other helping and being helped experiences. This baseline is then used to plan individual educational and practice goals, consistent with course expectations and requirements.

The self-positioning method can be used in specific ways at other critical points during training, for example for college re-entry after a block placement, as well as during the student's future career. We are concerned here with its relevance for practice placements. A successful outcome of the initial period of self-positioning would be for a student to be thinking actively about his aims for his practice placement(s) and to be discussing these regularly with his tutor and peers, alongside his academic studies and other course experiences. In this way he will be well prepared for the stages of making placement arrangements and preparing for the supervision relationship.

Detailed general preparation in college for entering a placement and taking up the student practitioner and supervisee roles can be organised on either a block (say, one week) or a spread out basis. A typical programme might have four components:

(1) *A review of course work on knowledge, skills and values* The focus would be on each student's current level of understanding, skill and attitudes, and on the implication of this for his placement agenda and contract.

(2) *The administrative knowledge and skills* needed for a particular placement, including understanding of agency policy and

procedures, and preparation for recording and workload management.
(3) *Clarification and discussion of the assessment procedures, methods and standards.*
(4) *Developing learning and self-management skills* As these 'process' skills may be less obvious than the other three areas, and as they are central to the supervisee role, we shall now consider each in some detail.

*Learning skills*
When the placement approaches, and with the benefit of feedback from tutors, fellow-students and any previous practice-teachers, the student should have some idea of his own learning-style (see Chapter 2). He may wish to extend this style in new directions, for example to develop a capacity for thinking before rushing into action.

He will need to be prepared for the 'normality' of feeling self-conscious in his work with clients, and to understand that, like learning to drive a car or attempting any new skill, the self-conscious stage precedes the assimilation of the skill into a more 'natural' way of behaving. It is also normal to experience fluctuations in progress and development during a course, and during placements, and this will be understood by the perceptive practice-teacher and tutor.

An essential aid to learning is *retention of relevant information*. In addition to recording for supervision and agency purposes the student needs to develop the habit of carrying a notebook everywhere in which he jots down (as soon as possible after each event), in personal diary style, all relevant information, experiences, and feelings, and also questions (practical, technical, intellectual and philosophical) which may arise. The reason for this is that our conscious memory only retains a small proportion of the information it receives, and these notes will be invaluable to the student for a range of purposes including: preparation of official records and reports, preparation of material for supervision sessions, case-material and issues for discussion in seminars at the college or in student-unit groups, and as a resource for personal thinking and reflection.

The student will not usually want to read theory 'cold' during placement, but he can be encouraged to use the literature and information sources when particular problems or obstacles are faced in his practice, e.g. a student with little experience of alcoholism may find himself working with a family with an alcoholic member. This is likely to motivate him to seek out the relevant literature, perhaps after consultation with his practice-teacher or tutor, and as a resource to be used selectively rather than prescriptively.

*Self-management skills*

There is much that can be done to help the student prepare himself for professional self-management on placement and for the supervision relationship. At Bristol we have identified several areas which students are encouraged to think about individually and in groups, in response to key questions. These are:

(1) *What role-changes are likely to be important for you when you start on placement? What will your title be?* Many students have to make multiple role-changes during training, e.g. prior to the course a student ran his own small business and worked for some years as a volunteer with the Probation Service. He is about to start a placement as a trainee probation officer and needs to prepare for both the role-change from volunteer to professional social worker, and 'officer of the court', and from being 'managing director' to Trainee Probation Officer. He needs to alert his practice-teacher to the major adjustments he must make, and seek her help in facing the transition and in trying to avoid inappropriate behaviours based on previous roles.

(2) *Do you think it matters how you dress and present yourself, on placement, to clients, colleagues, practice-teacher and others?* Discussion of this might include possible conflicts between student preference (perhaps for jeans and informality), client expectations (variable), practice-teacher views (variable?) and agency expectations (e.g. to look 'respectable' and – for men – to wear a suit and tie in court).

(3) *Is it wise to self-disclose personal information early on in the placement (a) to your practice-teacher, and (b) to clients?* Each student will have a natural style on self-disclosure which, with help, he can locate on a continuum between the two extremes of 'complete reticence' and 'letting it all hang out'. He can be alerted at this preparatory stage to the significance his self-disclosing style may have in his work-relationship with both practice-teacher and clients. One of his objectives for the placement might be to refine the content and timing of self-disclosure.

(4) *What place, if any, do your personal beliefs/values/politics have in your work on placement?* This is another facet of the management of the personal–professional boundary and students sometimes get into conflict with practice-teachers for letting their personal ideology influence their practice. Some open sharing (by the practice-teacher also) early on in the placement can be very helpful.

(5) *In what ways, if any, do you think you may be a threat to your practice-teacher and/or others in the agency?* Students often underestimate the impact that their impending arrival has on their practice-teacher (particularly the inexperienced and first-timers). They are encouraged to empathise with their practice-teacher and to be aware that she may be anxious and threatened by the arrival of a student 'with all the latest ideas', and by the anticipated exposure of her own work and behaviour. This kind of awareness may reduce the incidence of student–practice–teacher versions of the games-playing referred to earlier (see Chapter 2).

(6) *Do you think you should seek help on placement whenever you feel the need? If so, from what source?* This question alerts the student to the issue of dependency and its management. It is expected that dependency will be high in the initial stages, but that this will reduce as the placement proceeds. The student may need to discuss with his practice-teacher the basis of informal contact and accessibility, and also the extent of his freedom to consult with other staff as the need arises. Part of the skill of the student supervisee is to study his practice-teacher's work programme and availability and to accumulate information about the range of other resources available to him in the agency.

(7) *If you feel critical of aspects of agency practice, what should you do about it?* This is a dilemma for a student, not least because of his quasi-guest role and because his work is being formally assessed by a member of the agency. He can be helped to anticipate the possible eventuality, to be aware that client interests and needs are primary, and to avoid impulsive actions at an early stage before he has established his own credibility. An extreme example of impulsive action was displayed by one student who, on the third day of his placement wrote to the Chief Probation Officer to complain about the way the Probation Service entries appeared in the local telephone directory! A contrasting, and fortunately rare occurence is when a student on residential placement observes violence by staff against residents. He needs to be aware of the key roles his practice-teacher and tutor can play in talking it over and deciding

whether some form of action should be taken, especially if he approaches them sooner rather than later. In my experience, many students are reluctant to approach tutors about difficulties (of whatever kind) on placement, but usually find it helpful when they find the courage to do so.

(8) *In what roles may you be cast by agency staff?* This question highlights the entry of the student into an interactional system in which he may face influences and pressures from staff and find himself cast in roles such as 'dogsbody', expert, ally, scapegoat, consultant and sounding-board. He will have to be active, and on occasion, confronting, if he does not wish to accept the proferred role.

(9) *How do you plan to manage any stress which you may experience on placement?* It is helpful to the student to anticipate the various stresses he may experience and to generate ideas for coping. There is *anticipatory stress* which can be debilitating; but which generates the anxiety necessary for good work performance. This stress is best reduced by activity, and should disappear when the placement begins. There is the *initial stress* after starting placement, generated by all the new stimuli, relationships and learning. This can be reduced by planning periods of 'time-out', by noting down the various tasks and demands, and working out priorities. Simulations and exercises, for example on workload management, can facilitate this coping skill.

A third area of potential stress is the *uncertainty of the task*, and the difficulty of evaluating achievement. When morale and positive reinforcement is low at work, compensatory achievement in other areas of the student's life can be an important sustaining influence. There may also be *stresses in the agency environment*, due to organisational and staff-changes, resource-problems, pay or working conditions' disputes, or other factors. This can be very unsettling for both student and practice-teacher, but may be reduced by concentrating on the needs of clients.

## Preparation for a specific placement

*Selection of placement* Courses and agency staff often have to balance a student's learning needs against his personal circumstances when seeking a suitable placement. Syson's research indicated that non-recognition of personal factors could adversely affect placement experience. It is important, therefore, that the student identifies clearly both his professional and personal needs as he seeks to influence placement selection, within the limits of negotiability.

*Contact with the potential practice-teacher* A pre-placement, preliminary meeting between student and potential practice-teacher is essential before placement arrangements are confirmed and a placement contract negotiated. This crucial encounter is an opportunity to explore aims, methods and attitudes, and most importantly, to test for mutual compatability. An early meeting is desirable because whilst most such meetings establish rapport and a sound basis for future work together, there are occasions when serious difficulties emerge, and an alternative placement may be needed.

*The placement contract (or agreement)*
The three-way meeting of student, practice-teacher and tutor, which needs to take place before the placement starts or soon afterwards, is a special version of the consultancy and supervision contracts discussed earlier. It is of great importance for the student, especially on a final placement, because this meeting and the document which records it, provide explicit information about the terms of the placement. The student therefore needs to be well prepared and confident enough to express his views and needs. A typical contract would cover the following areas:

(1) *Aims of the placement*
The general aims for all placements and students will be outlined in a course document. The specific aims for *this* student in *this* placement context need to be discussed and agreed, for example a student who has difficulties coming to terms with his own authority might set a specific aim 'to develop skills and confidence in the use of authority with clients'.
(2) *Timing and structure*
Working hours, holidays; time for reading, study and projects; dates for discussion and submission of evaluation reports . . .
(3) *Work to be undertaken* (quantity and quality)
Amount of work; range and types of client/problem; social work methods, skills, techniques; statutory/office duties; observation; shared work . . .
(4) *Supervision and teaching*
Arrangements for supervision sessions; types of supervision methods, for example live-supervision, role-play; others involved in supervision/teaching/assessment/consultancy . . .

(5) *Tutoring during placement*
    Role and general availability of tutor; task, frequency and format of three-way meetings; access to student's work, for example tapes, records . . .
(6) *Assessment*
    Clarification of course procedures; methods to be used; roles of student, practice-teacher and tutor in assessment . . .
(7) *Accommodation and secretarial help*
(8) *Role of student in the agency*
    Attendance at staff-meetings, title . . .
(9) *Feedback and support for practice-teacher*
    Consultation available to practice-teacher, feedback to and from tutor.

With good preparation, a contract meeting of this kind may take about two hours. With poor preparation and/or special factors, more than one meeting will be needed. It is time well spent.

The contract does not have legal status, but it is an important document recording the professional agreement of the participants. It is to be taken seriously, but not rigidly, as circumstances may change and revision be needed. It offers student and practice-teacher a clear baseline and checklist, useful to return to at review points or when difficulties arise.

*Preparation by the practice-teacher*
Most textbooks on student supervision (e.g. Young 1967; Pettes 1979; Danbury 1979), emphasise the importance of careful preparation for the arrival of the student, and outline the steps to be taken. These preparations can be summarised under the three areas of agency context and resources, course context, and self.

*Agency context and resources* The student will be entering an organisation as well as an individual relationship with a practice-teacher, and the quality of his learning will depend greatly on whether he enters a facilitating or an alien environment. Part of the practice-teacher's task is to prepare team-members, team-leader, relevant managers, administrative, clerical and domestic staff and so on, for his arrival. In residential and day-care settings the student will enter a living community of residents/day-clients, and they need to have relevant information, suitably communicated, about the student's impending arrival. In multi-disciplinary settings such as hospitals and child-guidance clinics, the other professions need to be prepared, as do court personnel in probation, and local committees in voluntary and community agencies. It can make so much difference to the anxious 'new' student to feel welcome and expected in the first days and weeks.

The student will need various resources which the practice-teacher may have to negotiate and obtain from the agency. These include suitable accommodation (a personal space, however small, is essential), use of telephone, secretarial and dictation arrangements, information about agency procedures, stationery, and so on.

*Course context* The practice-teacher needs some understanding of the placement as part of a total learning experience offered by the college. This can be facilitated by attending meetings at the college, reading relevant documentation about the academic and structural components, as well as items relating specifically to the placement such as placement guidelines, manuals, and assessment procedures. The establishment of a working relationship with the relevant tutor prior to the contract meeting is useful.

*Self* There are various additional ways in which the practice-teacher can prepare professionally and personally. She should only agree to take a student if she has a positive motivation and an interest in the task. She needs to create the necessary personal space for the student in her own work programme, and this should (but often does not) include a reduced workload in recognition of an additional time-consuming and responsible task.

She needs basic information about the student and the placement requirements, to help her in planning for the initial workload and tasks which the student will undertake – the detail of this needs to await the contract negotiations with tutor and student.

The personal preparation is akin to that suggested for all consultants, including the personal reflection on motivation, attitudes and feelings about the task ahead, and acknowledgement of any prejudices likely to influence supervision and assessment. For example, the basic information about a student's age, previous education and occupations, race, sex, marital status, will have its impact, and fantasies need to be tested against the real person.

The new practice-teacher may need to remind herself to focus on the student's anxiety rather than her own(!) and the experienced practice-teacher to remember not to underestimate the newness for the student of the supervisory experience with which she is now familiar.

The student unit supervisor, with a full-time job of training students, has a role which in some ways is more akin to that of the tutor than to that of social workers who take students in addition to a practice workload. Space does not permit an examination of the special features of the student unit and the unit supervisor's task, and the reader is referred to Curnock's research study (1975).

*Preparation by the tutor*
The personal tutor's task is to help the student to make his individual path through the various preparatory stages, including selection and confirmation of placement, and to inform herself (preferably by visiting) about the practice context which the student will be entering. The tutor can facilitate the continuity of the student's learning experience, especially as he moves to and fro across the college-placement boundary. She also has a special responsibility to monitor the evaluation of the student's practice.

**Placement learning and supervision**
A few selected areas will now be considered:

*Preparation for supervision sessions*
When supervision sessions are used actively by the student they can provide a rare opportunity to get detailed feedback on work performance, personal style and professional development. This is much more likely to occur if the student prepares actively, generates questions which have been thought out beforehand, is able to take a share of the control of the meeting, and feels free to make his needs known. Part of his skill is to facilitate the practice-teacher's own performance in their interpersonal transactions. As stated previously, practice-teachers are human beings who have needs too, for example for positive reinforcement, and who have diverse strengths which the student needs to discover and use to maximum advantage.

With preparation along the lines suggested in the preceding pages the student will have started this process when negotiating the placement agreement, thus securing a firm foundation for an active learning experience.

**Visible practice**
Whereas in residential work the professional practice of staff is inevitably mostly visible to colleagues and others, in fieldwork it has traditionally been largely if not entirely invisible. This has been reflected in student fieldwork practice in which, typically, the practice-teacher has relied on indirect evidence of the student's work, and principally the student's own written and verbal

accounts. Incredibly, most fieldwork placement evaluation still relies overwhelmingly on indirect (Syson 1981, p.148), and therefore sometimes inaccurate, information. We shall identify some of the reasons for this strange phenomenon, indicate trends towards increased visibility, and review a range of ways in which students and practice-teachers can obtain first-hand information about the student's work which can both facilitate the student's learning and be used for assessment purposes.

Historically, the absolute privacy of the worker–client relationship has been a sacrosanct ethical principle governing fieldwork practice. This important ethic of confidentiality, however, is often undermined by the accessibility to many staff (but usually not the client himself) of the written record of these 'private' encounters, and it also sometimes appears to be affording protection for the social worker whose quality of work is not open to scrutiny or challenge by peers, supervisor or other clients. Many practice-teachers were themselves trained, and have subsequently practised on the 'invisible' model, and so have not been accustomed to their own practice being observed by colleagues or their supervisors. They do not therefore have much if any personal experience of participant consultancy linked to visible practice, and may resist, overtly or covertly, training-course pressures to develop a more open approach to student practice and evaluation. On the student side, their understandable anxiety about exposing their work to their practice-teacher and others is reinforced by the lack of opportunity to observe these experienced practitioners in action. Thus many practice-teachers model privacy and non-disclosure, and may justify it on various grounds, including confidentiality. Important changes are occurring however, so that the generalisation I have just made (which is amply supported by Syson's research and my own experience of numerous student placements) no longer applies to an increasing number of practitioners and practice-teachers, for the following reasons:

Firstly, the team concept in social work practice is developing, with practitioners giving much more attention to working together, not only on administration, work-allocation and case-discussion, but also in joint and shared work with their clients, whether individuals, families, small groups or communities. What they have discovered is that not only does this often provide a better use of resources and a better service to the client, but it also provides a support-structure for staff, in which colleagues gain strength from one another rather than being undermined and threatened as they had feared.

Secondly, the development of a range of methods of working with clients in groups, often requiring two or more workers, for example intermediate treatment programmes, family therapy, enables visible practice to develop naturally and less self-consciously (a pattern familiar to residential staff).

Thirdly, there is a continuing and changing shift in the emphasis of casework, with individual therapeutic work and counselling now being only one among several approaches which include advocacy, social-skills training, problem-solving methods and community-orientated social work.

Fourthly, training and consultancy techniques (of the kind described earlier in this text) have been developed which depend on tape-recordings, direct observation, joint work and participatory supervision, all of which offer visible practice and the potential for direct feedback, learning and evaluation.

Confidentiality is of course still very important, but it seems that provided safeguards for the client are observed, and practitioners behave in a professionally responsible way, many clients are more concerned about getting effective help than obtaining total privacy. The use of contracts is one way of ensuring that the basis of confidentiality is agreed and understood.

These developments are gradually creating more favourable conditions for visible student practice. All the techniques described in Chapter 1 as participant and observed consultancy can be used in student supervision. As a generalisation, the more confident the practice-teacher is in their use, the less anxious the student (and the clients) will be.

*Example*:
One student, low in self-confidence, undertook a placement where part of his work was with a psychiatric outpatient interdisciplinary team using a family therapy approach with a one-way screen and live supervision. He was very apprehensive at first, and this was reinforced by the traumatic experience of his first family walking out of treatment early on in his first observed session! He received vital support from the supervisory team, and several months later when the placement ended he had become an active and enthusiastic member of this working-group, taking 'supervisor' as well as supervisee roles, and finding the experience of direct feedback and support a great help in improving both his skills and his self-confidence. There is little doubt that the role-modelling of practice-exposure and risk-taking by his practice-teacher and the other experienced workers, plus the opportunity to be supervisor as well as supervisee, contributed to this positive learning experience.

When practice-teacher and student undertake some form of joint work it is essential that roles are clarified so that both of them and the client(s) know how they will be working together. The range of possibilities extends from the student being in the primary role, with the practice-teacher occasionally participating, through work as co-equals, to the practice-teacher as primary worker with the student in a clearly defined assistant or apprentice role. The reality of such joint work is often less threatening than the anticipation, and frequently practice-teachers and students will say that it turned out to be much more productive than they had expected. What is not helpful is 'one-off' joint work which puts undue pressure on the participants (very often including the client), with the disproportionate weighting of one shared episode making it counterproductive, and perhaps atypical.

It needs to be recognised that working with your assessor observing your work (and it can feel like observation even when there is joint participation) can be a pretty un-nerving experience for most of us, and this is especially likely when there is incompatability or lack of trust. It is strongly recommended that students seek, and are offered, some additional experiences of joint work with other students and/or practitioners, who are briefed to give feedback to aid the student learning. There is much to be gained from working with a range of people on placement, provided the status of the co-worker, vis-à-vis assessment, is clarified. I return to both of these points shortly.

*Tape-recordings*
These are useful tools for both learning and assessment, but their use is surrounded by anxieties, some more rational than others. It is essential that client confidentiality is protected, and there must always be full consultation and agreement beforehand. What I have observed is that there is often a direct correlation between the attitude of practice-teacher and student, *and* between the attitude of the student and his clients when permission is sought. There are many ways of communicating one's views and feelings! Some students are excessively anxious about tape-recording their work, irrespective of their practice-teacher's attitude. One way of easing into it is to agree that the first couple of tapes are for the student only, and that practice-teacher and tutor will only listen to later ones. What almost inevitably happens when the student plucks up courage and starts taping is that he feels very positively about it afterwards because of the benefit to himself of direct feedback on his practice.

*Example*:
One student did not realise until he heard himself on tape, that he sometimes cut across what the client was saying, by making interjections himself instead of really listening to what the other person was saying. He was then able to rectify this in a subsequent interview and to hear, *for himself*, how much he had improved.

This kind of self-learning often occurs with tape-recordings, and is very effective, but it can be further enhanced by the practice-teacher helping the student to pick out key learning points and to identify ways of refining his skills, e.g. in the example given, the practice-teacher gave feedback on the listening problem as it also affected supervision sessions, and she devised listening exercises to facilitate the improvement.

Taped inverviews of how the student *actually* works with people are also important for assessment purposes, but with the same proviso as that given for joint work, that the pressure is much reduced when the method is used often rather than occasionally.

The interests and rights of the clients must be protected at all times, and the student can be helped, for example by rehearsal and role-play, with the skill of explaining the use of a tape to clients, negotiating with them, and if they agree, making a clear mini-contract about the confidentiality of the contents. It is of course quite unsuitable for some clients and some methods of working.

## *Sharing student supervision*

Discussion so far has concentrated on the student–practice-teacher pair as the locus of learning, supervision and assessment. I would now like to qualify this by emphasising the value for the student of opportunities to consult with other social workers, individually and in groups. Just as social work practice is being enriched by broadening the work unit from one-to-one casework to include other clients and other workers, similarly the student's learning experience can benefit from exposure to a range of work-styles attitudes and expertise. There are two pre-conditions. Firstly, the named practice-teacher retains a central role and responsibility in the consultancy 'network', and secondly the status of information about the student's performance which is passed from other staff to the practice-teacher is made clear. Practice-teachers inevitably get informal feedback from others (including team-members, managers, clerical and domestic staff) which influences their assessment, but is not always explicit and known to the student. The contract should cover this point, and the student should know that the content of such feedback *will* be one of the factors influencing his final assessment.

One stage further is when a specific piece of supervision and assessment is formally delegated by the practice-teacher to a specialist colleague. Examples of this might be divorce-court welfare supervision in Probation, adoption supervision in Social Services, and groupwork supervision in a residential setting. The 'second' supervisor needs to provide a written report covering that specialist piece of work, and to be available to discuss it with practice-teacher and student.

A variation on shared supervision is the 'linked placements' model described by Davis and Walker (1982). In this approach a student is based in one agency setting, but formally linked to one or more others that deal with some of the same clients. The authors give an example of a student based in a hospital student unit, who was enabled to work with a client in the three settings of hospital, area team and a voluntary agency rehabilitation centre. The supervisory arrangements in the area team were agreed beforehand, but the student was able to negotiate his own role and supervision in the rehabilitation centre. This model, which depends on permeable agency boundaries, enables students to follow and parallel their clients' experience of contact with residential, day-care and community settings in the same area. It fits well with a systems and network perspective, and is suitable for a final placement student who can take some responsibility for negotiating his own work and directions.

## Applying theory to practice

Social work students are frequently told that they should be applying their recently acquired theoretical knowledge on their practice placement. Syson's research (pp.100-105), following the Stevenson–Parsloe findings (1978, p.339), confirmed that most of the time, on most placements, this does not happen, at least consciously or explicitly. This state of affairs is so ubiquitous that structural explanations beyond the immediate practice-teacher–student pair are needed. Such explanations might include the bifurcated structure of social work education and training, the inadequacies of the theories and their academic proponents, the complexity of the practice context, the atheoretical stance of many practitioners, and misconceptions about how people learn. These are all major topics, and I shall make just two observations.

Theories, including practice-theories, can influence general understanding, perspectives and approaches, but it seems they are not much help to the practitioner in his day-to-day work. What he also needs are *skills and techniques which he can use*. Social work courses have only recently begun to include in their curricula coherent skill-development sequences (Lewis and Gibson 1977) in which students can learn, rehearse and refine basic skills such as engaging the client, listening, clarifying, purposeful interaction, contracting and ending. This learning can be acquired both prospectively and retrospectively to enhance practice competence (to which it needs to be closely linked), and early indications are that students can 'apply' it because it has experiential meaning for them. It has become part of them.

Another problem for students, is that their teachers (tutors and practice-teachers) sometimes have not developed an integration of theoretical understanding and practice-skill for themselves, and in effect the student is being required to achieve a more advanced stage of integration than his mentors! This is not impossible, but the student can learn much faster when he has suitable role-models.

*Evaluation and assessment of practice*
This chapter has focused on the learning component of practice-placements, but with periodic reminders of the practice-teacher's dual role as teacher and assessor. There has been widespread dissatisfaction with the general quality of practice assessment, and a series of journal articles in recent years (Brandon and Davies 1979; Davies 1979; Morrell 1979 and 1980; Parsloe and Stevenson 1979; Curnock and Prins 1982) have alerted the profession to the urgent need to improve its methods of assessment.

Two of the areas already discussed are directly relevant to improved assessment. These are (a) clear placement and assessment guidelines, and an explicit placement contract, and (b) first-hand evidence of visible practice by the student. A third factor is the capacity of practice-teachers and tutors notwithstanding the close working relationships they develop with students, to be able to make fail recommendations. As Morrell (1980) and others have pointed out the requirement must be the positive one that the student should demonstrate competence, rather than the negative one of avoiding gross incompetence. Supervision should include evaluative feedback throughout the placement so that indications of potential failure are communicated to the student at an early stage. One of the advantages of visible practice is that the practice-teacher can quote relevant data or point it out on a video or audio recording in a much more convincing way than she can when evaluating indirectly. No-one likes to fail, but most students, at least in theory, recognise that standards must be upheld and a 'licence to practice' must really mean something which offers both protection and good service to the client.

**Self-management in the social worker role**
To consolidate the proactive philosophy towards the end of training, courses can offer specific preparation for self-management in the first few months as a practitioner-employee. Simulations, exercises, role-plays, discussions and visits from agency staff can all be used to prepare for managing a work-load, using supervision and consultancy, working in a team, working in an organisation and inter-agency/inter-professional collaboration. A major emphasis is on the skills of negotiation and managing the tensions of influencing and being influenced. Elsewhere (Brown 1981), I have described one such course which attempts to do this.

# 5 Group Consultancy

This chapter is concerned with consultancy in a group context. The first section is about the use of group approaches as the *means* of achieving aims similar to those of individual consultancy and supervision. The second section is about staff group consultancy when the focus is on the *working group itself*, and those group issues which influence the way the task is carried out.

## A group approach to consultation and supervision

'Group supervision can offer an opportunity for a supportive community whose norms of mutual aid and client service permit only the best in practice to develop' (Abels 1977).

The essence of this model is a group setting in which several workers meet together, by arrangement and often with a designated leader, to consult with each other on practice issues which they are encountering in their work. (*Note*: In a group model the minimum number of consultees is three, provided each brings separate pieces of work for consultation. If two co-workers bring the same piece of work, more than one other worker is required to get the range of contributions that a group can offer.)

In Chapter 1 we identified the three main versions of this model, and they are briefly summarised again here:

(1) *Group Supervision* is when a supervisor meets with some or all of her supervisees for supervision on a group basis. The composition of the group is largely determined by role, that is supervisor and supervisees, and membership may be compulsory or by negotiation. When all members of a team meet together in this way it is sometimes called *team supervision*. Consistent with the focus of this book, our interest here is in the consultancy-like functions of group supervision, not the administrative-managerial functions, except when the latter directly influence the former.

(2) *Facilitated group consultancy* is when a group of workers meet on a voluntary basis for mutual consultation, with a designated leader or facilitator who is not their supervisor. They are usually brought together by some common professional interest, such as fostering and adoption, residential work with the elderly, intermediate treatment, the use of volunteers.

(3) *Peer group consultancy* is a mutually consulting peer group, a self-help group with no designated leader. There may on occasion be an organiser (see Fizdale 1958), but the group is the collective responsibility of the members. The composition of the group is likely to be determined by a combination of a shared work interest and personal affinity. The members are often at a fairly similar stage of professional skill and understanding, for example four relatively young recently-appointed Senior Probation Officers meeting regularly for six months to offer each other consultancy and support in their new role.

Of these three versions only group supervision carries direct organisational accountability

Group models, which may be particularly attractive to those who like working in and with groups, share many of the characteristics of groupwork practice models. These include:

*Preparation*
Consultancy groups are no exception in being dependent for their success on thorough preparation. This includes not only pre-group negotiations between the members and the leader, but also the establishment of collaborative relationships with other relevant agency staff to ensure a facilitating rather than a hostile environment for the group. This is especially important in residential work where all group meetings are highly visible, inclusion and exclusion are highlighted, and some colleagues have to keep the establishment going whilst others do their consulting.

*Group Composition and Size*
Consultancy groups will be profoundly influenced by the extent to which the members already know each other. Some groups with members drawn from a wide catchment area, and perhaps different agencies, will have the properties of stranger-groups, and much attention in the early stages will need to be given to group formation, trust and cohesion. At the other extreme is group supervision for members of a team who may have been working together for several years. This group will have some properties similar to those of a natural group, such as the family, with set patterns of communications and role-expectations, and probably some taboo topics.

Consultancy groups may be *open* (changing membership) or *closed* (fixed membership). A closed group often enables trust and cohesion to develop quicker, but with the possible danger in long-term groups of becoming inward-looking and stale. Open groups bring in new members with new ideas, but the group has the additional task of coping with a series of joinings and leavings. If these changes are frequent there is a risk of instability and discontinuity.

The *optimum size* relates to the degree of homogeneity of members' interests. Within the range of, say, four to ten members, the larger size will be more successful if the members' interests and consultancy aims are fairly similar. If they are very disparate, the opportunity for 'resonance' and lateral learning is reduced, and a smaller group (or no group) is to be preferred.

*Contract*

The group will need to agree on its task, structure, process and methods of working. All the contract meeting agenda items outlined (in Chapter 2) for individual consultancy, will be relevant with the added dimension of working out how the group can meet the separate but related interests, needs and aims of the different members.

*Stages of Development*

A consultancy group which is newly formed will experience changes over time which are characteristic of all formed groups. One of the simplest and best known models is Tuckman's (1965) 'Forming, Storming, Norming and Performing' to which 'Ending' (or 'Mourning') was added later. These stages represent: an initial period of group formation, a subsequent testing of the group as members seek roles within it, a period of cohesion and productivity, and a termination phase. These stages apply to each group session as well as to the life-span of a group. Development over time may also have cyclical, or regressive phases, caused by changes of various kinds, for example groups which gain and lose members periodically, as in group supervision, have to *re*form to adjust to changing membership. Consultancy group leaders and members need to understand the developmental stages of their own group if it is to be an enabling vehicle for its members.

*Process and Task*

The quality of the working relationships and group culture established in a consultancy group will influence the achievement of individual and collective tasks. As in any other group the skill of the leader and members lies in creating a group process which facilitates the work. In group supervision where members may come initially under some duress, the establishment of trust and confidence in the group and in the supervisor will be essential if the work is to be done effectively, and congenially.

## Programme

A consultancy group needs some agreement on *how* it will carry out its task. This includes decisions on how to allocate time between the interests of different members, how much flexibility there will be to adapt a plan to meet changing and urgent needs, and what kinds of methods are to be used, such as discussion, role-play, sculpting.

*Example*:
A consultancy group with a groupwork focus has a facilitator and eight members, who are four pairs of co-leaders. The client groups they are working with are diverse: a social skills group for teenage girls on supervision orders, a support group for recently divorced and separated people, an information and assessment group for prospective foster-parents, and a back-pain group. Each of these groups is different in its membership, aims and approach, but the common factor is that all are time-limited formed groups with co-leaders. They all need to develop programmes and ways of working to enable them to achieve their aims in a relatively short time.

The consultancy method used is an adaptation of Maple's (1977) 'shared decision-making' model. Nine fortnightly two-hour meetings are arranged, the first being a shorter contract-making meeting. It is agreed that each session will begin with a brief joining and information-sharing period (15 minutes). There will then be two 45-minute periods, in each of which one pair takes the consultee role (by prior arrangement) and presents issues from its groupwork on which it wants consultancy help. Examples of issues are: how to run a first session, how to include a silent member, how to develop collective responsibility. During that 45-minute period the other seven people are all in the consultant role. The final quarter of an hour is left free for discussion of any outstanding issues from the other two pairs, and for future planning. Flexibility is built into the format, so that if one non-presenting pair has a major need which is more urgent than that of another presenting pair, the former can replace the latter, by agreement, or the middle section can be used for three 30-minute sessions. The initial information sharing is designed to pick up this kind of need, and a group culture develops in which all participants learn how to share the time in the most useful way.

The group facilitator usually finds that at the beginning members tend to look to her to respond to the issues raised. The leader skill is to draw in the other members very quickly, establishing the culture that when one pair presents all the others are consultants. Technically, the leader is enabling the group to move quickly from being leader-directed to member-directed (so that if, for instance, she is absent the group can function well without her). The member role, when not presenting, is to exercise leadership by focusing on the presenters' issues, and using consultant skills to help them. This is not a discussion group, and other members bring in their own experience only when it can contribute to the presenters' own issues and needs. The other group members are now working as a team and need to be careful not to bombard the presenters with too many questions, comments and suggestions, leaving perhaps two or three to take the main responsibility at any given time.

The presenters need to come well prepared with a clear idea of what they want help with, and how to communicate that to the group. They need to be aware also of their time-allocation and try not to intrude into another's space.

*The skills of the designated leader* in consultancy groups are very similar to those of the social groupworker (Shulman 1979; Brown 1979), and they can be summarised as *working with the group members to create a group culture of trust, cohesion and collective responsibility in which individuals are able to help each other with the problems and issues in their work which concern them.*

## The skills of membership in consultancy groups

The guidelines in Chapters 2 and 4 on being a proactive consultee and supervisee apply in consultancy groups. The crucial difference in a group is that the consultee takes the consultant role for much of the time, but always sharing it with others. It is in fact an excellent way of learning consultancy skills before taking a complete consultant role with full responsibility.

*Group supervision* has a potentially complex agenda including not only work consultation, but also administrative, supervisory and policy functions. One possible way round this is to have the same people (the team) having separate meetings for separate functions. In this way meetings for work consultation (focusing on members' work problems and skill development) are distinguished from meetings for other purposes such as work allocation, administration and staff evaluation. The supervisor using group supervision may face the problems of an involuntary group, one of indefinite duration and a group of slowly changing membership. The issue of *authority* is central, and the skill of the supervisor lies in winning the confidence and trust of her staff whilst staying in role as a line-manager. In group supervision she needs to be secure enough to delegate much of her leadership to her supervisees in their role as group-members, but not to the point of behaving as though she was in the same role-position as them.

In all consultancy groups, and group supervision in particular, there is the possibility of members getting stuck in roles such as scapegoat, silent member, monopolist, joker or deviant (yes, social workers can get into these roles just as easily as clients!). Most groupwork texts discuss ways of dealing with these phenomena, and Shulman (1982) makes suggestions specifically in the context of group supervision.

*In 'leaderless' peer-group consultancy*, members share between them the responsibility for the organisation and process of the group. This usually works best when key functions are identified, such as making practical arrangements, recording, convening a meeting, keeping time boundaries; and then allocated to different members, perhaps on some rotating basis. Both peer-groups and facilitated groups can *appear* to be an alternative power base and cause some anxiety to managers. Consultee group members have a responsibility to inform managers about what is happening and to ensure that agency accountability is suitably covered.

*Advantages of group consultancy*
*Mutual aid* is the core feature of the consultancy group. As in social groupwork, each member takes both the helper and helped role at different times. Shulman (1982) suggests several kinds of mutual aid: sharing information, testing different ideas, opening up taboo areas, the 'all in the same boat' feeling, mutual support and praise, mutual demand and mutual feedback.
*Problem-solving and lateral learning* In a group all members are learners and teachers, bringing a wide range of experience, understanding and ideas to bear on each individual's problem.
*An arena for simulation* Because of the numbers available, a group is a rich resource for consultancy methods like role-play, sculpting and rehearsal, which may need several people.
*Power-sharing, reduced dependency and egalitarianism* In a group, power and authority are shared more evenly whether the consultant-leader is a supervisor with delegated authority or an outsider with the authority of expertise and understanding. As Kaslow (1979) put it: 'I will argue that when the supervisor risks herself enough to deal with several workers simultaneously, the authority she exercises is more rational and less pervasive than in individual conferences . . .'

Other potential advantages of a group include support for each member's status as a competent worker, a socialisation process for new members (e.g. in team group supervision), a means to improved communication and, possibly, a more economical use of resources.

*Disadvantages*
*Competitiveness and conflict* may occur in any group because comparisons are inevitable, and are particularly likely in groups of supervisees if a parental style is adopted by the supervisor, evoking 'child' responses and sibling rivalry.
*Individual interests swamped by the group* There is a risk that this might happen especially in large or very heterogeneous groups if the individual (a) gets very limited opportunity to present his material, and/or (b) does not resonate with others and/or (c) is unable to generalise the learning from participating in the consultee work of others.
*Confidentiality and exposure* A group can be a threatening place, and some individuals may be apprehensive about exposing themselves, especially to close colleagues and when they fear their confidence may not be respected.
*The process 'trap'* There is a risk that a group, especially of people who know each other well, as in group supervision, may become so absorbed in their own process that it becomes akin to a sensitivity group, and the task of providing a better service to clients recedes into the distance.
*Organisational complexity* Any form of group meeting is more complicated to organise than one-to-one sessions because of the need to synchronise the availability of a greater number of people.

In summary, it is rather unhelpful to compare individual and group approaches as if they were mutually exclusively alternatives, because there is some evidence (Holder and Wardle 1980; H. Davies 1977) to support the impression than many workers prefer a combination of both individual and group opportunities for supervision and consultation. A research study comparing individual and group supervision for students (Sales and Navarre 1970) produced no significant differences in their skills and performance outcome.

Regarding evaluation of work performance, writers on group supervision differ on whether the function of individual evaluation should be group-based (sometimes called 'team assessment'). Getzel and Salmon (1982) suggest that whilst group supervision contributes to the formal evaluation process of supervisees, the 'actual formal evaluation of individual supervisees should be done individually to protect privacy and guarantee confidentiality'. Whatever approach is taken, both supervisees and supervisor need to know exactly what it is, avoiding any ambiguity.

Other points on group approaches:

*The consultancy/training/discussion group distinction* Consultancy groups can very easily slide into becoming training groups (with an emphasis on common learning points and general development), or discussion groups (when consultee and consultant roles are no longer distinguishable, specific pieces of work are no longer focused on, and a general exchange of views occurs). Both these modes will be present some of the time, but if they predominate it is no longer consultancy.

*Group consultancy and group supervision* Group supervision has many practical and administrative advantages as a setting for consultancy, and with a supervisor who is a skilled group-leader and supervisees with shared interests, it can be a very effective method. For experienced social workers with specialist interests, consultancy peer-groups with membership across teams and perhaps across agencies, for example family therapy consultancy groups, can be very stimulating and productive, whether used alongside or as an alternative to group supervision.

*Group supervision for students* Group supervision is particularly suited to student units because the homogeneity of role and relatively similar level of experience creates favourable conditions for a group approach (Davies 1977; Curnock 1975). Student participation in team group supervision can also be a rich source of learning.

## Staff group (or team) consultancy

We shall now focus on the work group. Social work is organised administratively in such a way that most social workers are combined with several other workers (not necessarily all social workers) in an identifiable work unit. These units have responsibility, on behalf of the agency, for providing a service to a defined constituency of clients, patients or customers. This grouping of workers, usually headed by a team-leader, unit head, senior or supervisor, is referred to variously as a work group, work unit, staff group or team. Staff group is used in the title of this section as an umbrella term, and to indicate the focus of this type of consultancy. The term, team, will however be used more often in what follows.

Several recent publications (Parsloe 1981; M. Payne 1982; C. Payne and Scott 1982) have useful and lengthy discussions about what defines a team, and about the different kinds of teams that exist, differentiated according to function, composition, setting and *modus operandi*. We shall try to side-step these complexities by thinking of teams loosely as groupings of workers who are expected to work together *at least* to the extent of coordinating their activity to ensure client needs are met and agency policy implemented. We noted earlier that teams vary along a continuum from the individualistic to the collective or collaborative, and in the degree to which they are leader or group directed. We should also differentiate three categories of team: *social work teams*, composed entirely of social workers; *social service teams*, composed of social workers and various other agency staff such as occupational therapists, social work assistants, clerical and domestic staff; and *multidisciplinary teams* composed of staff from two or more disciplines as in hospitals, child guidance clinics and other health settings. In the latter two categories there is frequently uncertainty about team-membership, (e.g. whether clerical staff are included) and this is often an issue in team consultancy.

The members of many work groups and teams, in both field and residential settings, spend much of their working week together, over long periods of up to several years. This results in group behaviour which is often more reminiscent of the family group and residential client groups than of either the typical stranger group of the laboratory or the short-term client group of the fieldwork setting. It is therefore important for anyone concerned with team-development and team consultancy to understand these features and their implications for any attempts to bring about change. These characteristics, which also derive from the organisational context, include:

(1) Having a task which is defined by the wider organisation or institution of which the work unit is a part, and being subject to the pressures and influences of that larger system.
(2) Being a long-term continuous group with a slowly (and sometimes quickly!) changing membership. Teams are only similar to formed groups when they are newly created by either a new organisation, like Social Services Departments in 1971, or by the restructuring of an existing organisation.
(3) Having a leader with designated authority over the other members, but one who is also part of the work group. Exceptions to this are some multi-disciplinary teams which do not

recognise a formal leader, for example some child-guidance clinics, and the occasional non-hierarchical collegiate team experiment, such as the Harlesden Community Project (1979).
(4) Group behaviours which are recognisable as those associated with different stages of group development, such as forming, storming, norming and performing (Tuckman 1965), but with a variable and fluctuating pattern created by the changing membership and the extent to which the work unit is truly a group (i.e. with significant interaction between the members) and not just an aggregate of individuals. Some 'teams' never get beyond the forming stage.
(5) The fixed roles characteristic of members of long-term groups, such as joker, placator, energiser, challenger, ideas-person, blamer.
(6) Having a past history which influences present functioning and attitudes to possible future changes.
(7) Having set patterns of communication, with tacit agreement about hidden agendas and 'no-go areas'.
(8) Having sub-groupings, alliances and unofficial power and status hierarchies, (age, length of service, sex, expertise, personality and so on).

These are the generalised characteristics which will vary in form and significance according to the unique features of each team context.

*The need for consultancy*
'Team-development should begin with a strong "felt need" to improve some basic condition or process that is interfering with the achievement of organisational goals.' This quotation is from Dyer's excellent book *Team Building* (1977), in which he makes the point that there needs to be clear evidence that the problem is internal and not external to the work group. A team may work out its own methods of assessment of need, or it may use questionnaires of the kind outlined by Dyer (p.36).

*Motivation for change*
It is one thing to identify a need, but quite another to develop the motivation to do something about it. Teams will often be divided on both the identification of need, and the willingness of members to do something to meet it. If the idea comes from one faction, say management, the other faction, say the workers, may be suspicious of ulterior motives, and *vice-versa*. An inherent paradox is that the

very conditions which create the need for change and help, i.e. conflict, poor communication, lack of effective joint work, lack of trust, apathy, problematic supervisor–supervisee relations, will often mitigate against change, and be effective barriers to help-seeking.

*Focus of change*
There are three possible arenas of change. One is the group *process* – all the issues associated with working together, communication, authority and power, relationships and so on. A second is the group *task* – all the issues associated with how the job is done. The third, and the one in which we are particularly interested here, is a combination of *process and task* in which the focus is on group process issues as they affect task-achievement.

*Is an outside consultant needed?*
If change is needed and desired, the work-group or team then has to decide whether to tackle the problems on its own ('do-it-yourself' consultancy) or whether to seek help from someone outside the team, either elsewhere in the agency, or externally. The following factors will be crucial to that decision, and the examples given under each heading are of conditions that indicate the need for outside help. (The converse in each case would be an indicator of favourable conditions for a self-help approach.)

(1) *The stage of group development* In the early stages of a team's life (or after several recent changes), when a team has got stuck at the forming/storming stages, or when a sudden in-team crisis occurs.
(2) *The attitude of staff to the supervisor* If there is conflict and lack of trust between staff and supervisor, and some evidence that the latter is part of the problem (in these circumstances outside help is essential).
(3) *The attitude and skills of the supervisor* If she is not happy about trying out something new with her staff, and/or she does not possess the necessary facilitation skills.
(4) *The quality of communication and honesty* If there are serious blocks to open and honest communication between members of the team.
(5) *Group culture, style and motivation* If the team is having major difficulties in establishing a suitable climate for change.
(6) *Team skills and resources* If the team feels it lacks the necessary skills and resources to tackle the issues unaided.

(7) *The extent of conflict and competitiveness* If the team is split by rivalries and tensions between individuals or sub-groups.

There is also the *feasibility* of being able to obtain, and if necessary pay, a consultant, although if the commitment is great enough, a way can usually be found.

**Self-help (do-it-yourself) models**
If the team conditions are generally favourable for self-help, two or three different approaches are possible:
*Use of special staff-meetings* These have the advantages of minimum disruption to work routines and client service, but the brief time available and lack of continuity can mitigate against any major development work.
*'Away-days'* An increasingly common practice in some Probation and Social Services Department field-teams is for the entire team to 'shut up shop' for a day and go to some other location to work in private at team issues. Field teams can plan for minimal staff cover at the office, but this is a much bigger problem for residential staff in units where a certain level of staffing is essential at all times. Nevertheless every effort should be made to involve all staff for at least some of the 'time-out' if this is at all possible.

Away-days vary in focus, methods and leadership. Agendas often include both process and task issues, usually in that order. Sometimes the supervisor/senior takes the formal leadership all day, in other teams overall responsibility for particular sessions is allocated to, or offered by, different staff members. Methods may include discussion, warm-up and trust exercises, sculpting, role-play and simulations. Some teams are very creative in planning their own programme, but those wanting help in devising a framework could turn to Dyer (1979, Chapter 6) where he lists various design options for the preparation, start-up, problem-solving/process analysis, feedback, action-planning and follow-up phases.

If a major focus is working relationships in the team, it is very difficult, if not impossible, for the supervisor to facilitate full and free exchange because she is part of the system, not outside it. Have you ever tried do-it-yourself family therapy?!
*Tandem-teams consultancy* is another possibility. The structure is a relatively simple one in which one team in the role of collective consultee presents issues, and the other team, functioning as collective consultant, tries to help the other resolve the problems. Next they reverse roles and reciprocate. The advantage of this approach is the opportunity for each team not only to benefit *qua*

consultee, but also in the consultant role each can gain insight into its own difficulties from observing the other's behaviour and struggles. The disadvantages, especially with larger teams, may lie in the complexity of the practical arrangements and the management of the sessions.

The success of any self-help model will depend on the willingness and ability of all team members to see themselves as facilitators of the group process and as helpers of the others as well as themselves. The difference from group supervision is the *group focus* of the work, with the supervisor being part of the target system and in a dual consultant/consultee role. This shared group membership can limit the effectiveness of self-help team consultancy, whereas an 'outsider' can sometimes be a powerful catalyst for change.

**Outside consultancy**

In discussing the role and skills of the outside consultant, we shall not repeat earlier discussion about the pros and cons of this person being an agency consultant or a complete outsider. First, a few examples will be given of situations in a variety of settings, all needing help from outside the staff-group.

*A Probation team* in which an older, long-serving Senior Probation Officer gets into frequent conflict with several of the younger, recently trained members of her team. These internal wranglings, exacerbated by sub-groups, alliances and competing factions, are adversely affecting the team's work programme and performance. In desperation, an external consultant is called in.

*A multi-disciplinary psychiatric unit in a general hospital.* Staff from the various disciplines of nursing, medicine, social work and occupational therapy wish to improve their collaborative work with patients and to understand each other's roles, skills and philosophies. A self-help group founders on the leadership issue and an external consultant is asked to help. (Note that this example has elements of *inter-group consultancy* which are not discussed separately here.)

*A crisis occurs in a residential home for children*, when a four-year-old boy reveals that a member of staff has been playing with him sexually. One staff-member is accused, and then another later commits suicide after leaving a confession-note. An external consultant (Len Davis, who reports this example in his book *Residential Care*, 1982) is called in to help the staff group to exorcise this trauma and renew their high-quality child care practice.

*A Social Services team.* A serious conflict has arisen over the team's approach to its work. Two recently trained members favour patch-based community methods, whereas others want to stick to traditional 'clinical' casework. It is realised that before the approach to the task can be discussed there is much work to be done on trying to reconcile competing philosophies. The senior does not feel able to lead such a discussion unaided.

*A few general guidelines* are now offered on how a consultant might approach situations of the kind just described:

'. . . most of the work goes into creating the role of being a consultant, and in dealing with the invitation, and once this problem is overcome the consultant from a family therapy orientation needs just then to be a family therapist'. (Street, 1981).

I would certainly agree with the first part of this quotation, but I would say that the skills of *both* the social groupworker *and* the family therapist are equally relevant to what is a special form of groupwork with a group which is rather like (but also very different from) a family.

The importance of the *contact* and *contract* stages has been emphasised throughout the book, and nowhere is this more crucial than in staff group consultancy. When an approach is made, often by a team-leader or a senior manager, on behalf of a total work-group, this is a promising start, but the commitment of all the members will need to be checked out directly with them at a preliminary meeting. Alternatively, an approach may be made by an individual who does not have a clear mandate from the whole group.

*Examples:*
A team-member approached a consultant on behalf of his peers, not having discussed it first with his supervisor. The consultant insisted that the supervisor be involved, but when approached by the team-member the supervisor was not willing to admit an outsider.

A consultant was approached by a head of a residential home who thought her senior staff needed to work at their personal relationships. They, perhaps with some justification, suspected her motives, and the consultancy did not even get to the contract stage.

These two examples illustrate the delicacy of the hierarchical component of the work-group, and the importance of the consultant sowing the seeds of a good working relationship with both supervisor and each individual member of the team. *One approach* is to meet all the potential participants individually pre-contract to assess individual attitudes, feelings and expectations. *An alternative* is to give each individual some space at an initial group meeting to share his feelings, and ideas in the presence of the others. This group approach has the advantage of modelling openness, but there are occasions when if there is a real breakdown in team relationships and perhaps fear of the more powerful members, a pre-contract individual stage may be necessary.

Some consultants think it important to form a special relationship with the most senior staff member, often the supervisor, because she has the most power to influence the consultancy. Maxwell Jones (1976) suggests that two key people in the group for the consultant to identify with and support are the authority-figure and the 'risk-taker'. I think that establishing credibility and acceptability with the supervisor (and indeed the risk-taker) is essential, but I would avoid a special relationship, or pairing, because this is likely to prejudice team-members' perceptions of the consultant's neutrality. Group consultants need to avoid getting 'hooked in' to any one individual in the group.

The main *contract* elements are similar to those in any type of consultancy, but special care needs to be given to establishing the following.

(a) *Who will constitute the staff-group?* In some contexts this is uncontentious, but frequently there is uncertainty, especially about the inclusion of high and low status staff, and temporary members such as students on placement. As a rough guideline inclusion is preferable to exclusion for anyone who is significantly involved in the immediate work-system, but there can be legitimate arguments for both including and excluding clerical and/or domestic staff.

(b) *What are the objectives of the consultancy?* Expectations, fantasies, hopes and fears need to be aired, and agreed aims established.

(c) *Methods of working* need to be explicit and acceptable to all. A special factor in staff-group consultancy is *the role to be taken by the consultant vis-à-vis the formal leader or supervisor of the staff-group*. One model is to have the team functioning with everyone including 'the boss' in their normal roles, and the consultant as a resource to the group, observing, commenting and advising. Alternatively it may be agreed that the consultant will be leading the consultancy sessions, at least in the early stages. What the consultant must *not* do is succumb to any pressures to take a quasi-managerial role. This must remain firmly with the managers. There is a close analogy here with family therapy, where the therapist must be careful to avoid undermining the role of the parent(s) in the family system.

## Early stages of consultancy

Having agreed on an overall objective and contract, the consultant needs to 'join' the work-group system by consolidating relationships with each individual and with the group-as-a-whole. The early task emphasis will be on obtaining and sharing information about the issues and any obstacles to change. The skill of the consultant lies in facilitating communication and trust in such a way that *new* data emerge which were previously hidden, masked or withheld. There are several ways of doing this, including: group discussion, questionnaires or sentence-completion exercises to be filled in individually and shared with the group; games or exercises to obtain symbols of the group's functioning, such as animal and machine metaphors; sculpting of the group to obtain different perceptions of group structure and relationships visually; team tasks, real or simulated, the undertaking of which may illustrate team dynamics. All these techniques are designed to obtain data for 'group-diagnosis' or problem analysis. In this and other phases, and particularly in larger groups, some work can be done in pairs and sub-groups.

## Problem-solving stage

It will already be apparent that I am suggesting the use of adapted group work and family therapy techniques, allied to a problem-solving model with a group focus. The approach to problem-solving will thus depend on the skills-orientation of the consultant, as well as the characteristics of the work-group and its identified problems. The common factor at this stage will be shifting the group preoccupation from problem-talking to change-options and ways of moving in the desired directions. This can be reinforced by individuals, sub-groups, or the whole group undertaking 'homework', attempting some agreed changes, and reporting back later with mutual feedback and discussion of progress. This is suited to a spread out model of consultancy sessions, as distinct from the block model, say two days together, which has certain other advantages like sustained impetus.

## Follow-up, review and evaluation

A follow-up meeting, say three to six months after the consultancy sequence ends, is a useful way of checking on progress and monitoring the impact of the consultancy intervention. The consultant *cannot*, however, control or insist upon the implementation of change.

It is quite a privilege to be asked to join a work-group as consultant, and the role of facilitator and mobiliser of individual and team resources can be very satisfying. It can also be very lonely at times. One problem is that those who most need outside help seldom seek it. The individual consultee skill lies in identifying team dysfunctioning and having the courage to alert colleagues and supervisor to the need to try and do something about it, painful as that may be. Few individuals and teams that take the risk regret it later.

# 6 Professional Development and the Team Context

The emphasis throughout this book has been on the consultation process (in and out of supervision) as a proactive means of enhancing the quality and effectiveness of the social work service to clients. It has also been recognised that an important but secondary aim is the increased job satisfaction, self-valuation and personal morale of the worker, all of which in turn are likely to contribute to his competence and his value as an agency resource.

In this final chapter the focus broadens to the *overall professional development* of the worker, including training, evaluation and general development, as well as consultancy and supervision, and to the *team context* where most agency services become operational. The career-long process of individual development will be influenced and fashioned by the task demands of the work context and the needs of team colleagues, as well as by the aspirations and special interests of the individual himself. For example, in the University Department where I work, we are constantly having to balance the professional development interests of an individual member of staff, as when researching and writing a book like this(!), with the needs of other colleagues, and most importantly, with the primary requirement of the job which is to help students learn to be social workers and to assess that learning. In any work context it is much easier to justify and obtain resources for professional development work when it can be demonstrated that this contributes to enhanced task-performance.

**The team context**
The social work team, or its equivalent, is the main context in which the consultancy, supervision and training components of staff-development are identified, and decisions made about how best they might be provided for from both inside and outside the team. Several interacting factors will influence these discussions and decisions. In outlining these below, there is an implicit preference for collaborative team models which rely quite heavily on group sharing and discussion as a basis for planning and decision-making.

(1) *Team composition*
Teams vary in size, composition and stability of membership. Each

of these variables will influence the team's functioning as a group, in ways familiar to students of group dynamics. Small teams (say six or fewer members) are likely to be characterised by intimacy, ease of organisation, vulnerability to loss or absence of members, and to be relatively limited in the range of ideas and resources. Large teams (say ten or more members) are likely to be richer in ideas, resources and flexibility, but more complex to manage, more susceptible to sub-groupings and to polarisation of roles. Composition will vary by age, sex, ethnicity, qualification, length of service, personality and attitudes. As in all small groups, a blend of homogeneity for stability and heterogeneity for vitality is desirable.

The characteristics of a team as a continuous group with a slowly (and sometimes quickly) changing membership were discussed earlier. A team with several quite new (but not necessarily inexperienced) members needs time to establish itself as a cohesive working group, and teamwork itself may be a major objective of staff-development for a period of time.

(2) *Team objectives*
Whatever a team's size, composition and stage of development as a group (and ideally these should be linked to objectives), its members are there to carry out a shared task. Agreement about objectives is therefore the potential common ground which can unite different team-members into an effective worker-group with a clear identity. The process of establishing team objectives, consistent with both agency requirements and client need, is often a slow process requiring many team discussions (perhaps partly on an 'away-day' basis, and perhaps with outside consultancy help) before broad agreement can be reached. Clarification of aims and methods provides a baseline for decision-making about staff development programmes at team and individual level.

(3) *Team resources (e.g. staff skills, strengths and styles)*
Most descriptive characteristics of team-members are quickly evident – age, sex, length of time in the team, amount of experience, and so on – but this is not so true of qualitative attributes. An important team task is to assemble an inventory of all the qualities, skills, special interests and work-styles which collectively the team has to offer. This information may be elicited by discussion and sharing, perhaps facilitated by some written questionnaires and peer feedback. (*Note*: the authenticity of peer feedback is increased when people have first-hand knowledge of each other's work.) The

outcome, set alongside the team's agreed objectives, should help the group to identify needs and gaps which indicate directions for professional development and post-qualification training. For example, it may emerge that a particular team has no-one who individually has plans to develop skills in recruiting and working with volunteers. If the team has identified this as a high priority for development, then one or preferably two members will need to develop the necessary skills, and be supported by their colleagues in taking whatever training steps are necessary.

(4) *The team-leader*
The person in this role, who works at the point where management and practice meet, is a key figure in any social work organisation, carrying as she does dual responsibility for the administrative supervision and professional development of staff. Parsloe (1981) and others (e.g. Barker and Briggs 1969) discuss the role and responsibilities of the team-leader overall, so we shall focus here on those variables which relate directly to the consultancy, supervision and professional development of social workers in the team.
*Bureaucratic-professional orientation* Team-leaders vary in the relative emphasis they place on the bureaucratic and professional components of their role. The more bureaucratically inclined will start with the needs of the organisation and the routinisation of policies and programmes for staff-development, linking them specifically to task commitment and administrative requirements. Consultancy may be viewed rather sceptically as a potential threat to the smooth-running, well-controlled team. Those with a professional bias will tend to start with the needs of clients, individual staff and the team, giving high priority to consultancy and training opportunities for staff. Their supervisory style is likely to be largely consultative, and they may underplay their managerial role.

Neither extreme is to be recommended, and in the long-term neither alone is likely to benefit team-members. The team-leader who is able to integrate her managerial and professional responsibilities will support teamwork, consultancy and staff-development, but always with an eye on task, objectives and service to clients as the yardstick for their initiation and evaluation. In focusing on consultation, this book has inevitably emphasised the professional components of supervision, but personal-professional interests need to be viewed continuously in their organisational context.
*Leadership-style and group-orientation* There are many facets of leadership-style–the autocratic-democratic *laissez-faire* continuum,

the instrumental-expressive balance and, the one selected for discussion here, the individual-group orientation. Group-centred team-leaders are those who are comfortable in groups, and who have training and experience in membership and leadership of groups. They are much more likely to emphasise group methods of working, both with staff and clients, than are their individualistic counterparts who, for whatever reason, have neither group leadership skills nor a group orientation. The former will favour open team-discussion of all issues, work hard to develop team cohesion, and be keen on group supervision and consultancy methods. The latter will keep group activities to a minimum, concentrating on individual supervision and individual programmes of staff development. The significance of this is, that however she approaches her task, the team-leader, consciously or not, is modelling group leadership, behaviours and attitudes which may get mirrored in the way team-members work with each other and with their clients. For example, one team-leader by enabling her staff to change, helped them to enable some of their clients to do likewise. Difficulties arise when either a group-centred leader has individualistically inclined team-members, or conversely. These are the kinds of conflict situation where an outside staff group consultant may be needed.

*Evaluation and feedback to staff* An integral part of supervision is staff appraisal and evaluation. The line-manager is expected to monitor standards and to ensure that agency tasks are carried out properly. Evaluation can also make a very important contribution to professional development. There are a range of ways in which the team-leader and the supervisee himself can build up the evaluation material, including joint work, live supervision, team assessment (in which all team members evaluate each other's work at periodic intervals), client feedback, written records and the worker's own self-evaluation. The essence of the process is that it furnishes the worker with information about his skills and personal style, which is likely to indicate directions for development, and the kind of consultancy and training opportunities he needs in the next phase of his development.

Even if formal inspection of standards is transferred from agencies to a new inspectorate (as recommended by the Barclay Report, 1982), internal evaluation and its contribution to staff development and increased competence will continue.

*The team-leader's own professional development* All that has been said about the social worker being proactive in identifying and fulfilling his own needs for consultancy and professional development applies equally to the team-leader. She will need to negotiate with *her* supervisor a programme of training and consultation (in and out of their supervisory relationship) and to seek evaluative feedback on her own work performance. She can also seek peer consultation and mutual learning by meeting with other team-leaders. All this should enhance her work as a team-leader and help her to keep her boundary-role between the team and management.

(4) *Team culture*
The goal to aim for is a team culture in which group trust and cohesion have been developed to a point where all feel able to share in a frank, honest and robust way their thoughts and feelings about the inter-relationship of their individual and collective needs, and what they can offer their clients. This type of culture does not just happen overnight. It requires much hard work over quite a long period, perhaps two years or more, and without a team-leader with group facilitation skills, it will be very difficult if not impossible to obtain.

(5) *Agency environment*
To paraphrase, 'No team is an island.' There is a real danger that in its efforts to become cohesive and collective, a team becomes isolationist, and competitive with other teams and the outside world. This may well be necessary for a while (and the active stimulation of inter-team competitiveness has a place) but any team which, long-term, seeks to meet all its needs internally, will become impoverished and restricted. Team-members need access to the consultancy and training resources available elsewhere in the agency, and beyond. To facilitate this process, the team-leader needs special skills in inter-group relations, and in negotiating across team and agency boundaries.

Staff development is gradually being recognised by agencies as a high priority, and there has, for instance, been a move in recent years to provide specific induction programmes for recently qualified staff. Check-lists are sometimes issued on appointment, enabling staff, with the help of their supervisor, to 'self-position' themselves against a range of tasks and competencies which they are expected to have reached after two years. This provides an agency framework for their negotiations and contracts with their supervisor and colleagues for a programme of supervision, consultancy and training. In Probation, the framework is set at regional level, with a staff development unit providing a programme across twelve or more agencies. This has the advantage of broadening the horizons of staff through the exchange of information, ideas and practices across agency boundaries.

## Programmes of Consultancy, Supervision, Evaluation and Staff Development

In summary, the following factors are seen to be crucial influences in the planning of professional development at individual and team level (for detailed examples relating differential supervision needs to the knowledge and skills required in residential and field teams, see Payne and Scott 1982).

(1) *Team objectives and the degree of agreement and commitment to them* (This is a pre-eminent factor, to which all others need to be related.)
(2) The knowledge and skills required to meet the needs of clients, and to do the job competently and creatively.
(3) The composition of the team, its stage of development and emerging culture.
(4) The role, style, skills and orientation of the team-leader.
(5) The collective staff development needs of team-members related to team objectives and the tasks they have to perform.
(6) The individual needs of team-members related to their stage of career-development.
(7) The consultancy and supervisory resources actually and potentially available inside the team, elsewhere in the agency, and externally.
(8) The training resources actually and potentially available in the agency, and externally.
(9) The priority and resources which agency management commit to staff development and to the *qualitative* improvement of professional practice and services to clients.

The professional requirements and needs of each worker and each team can be assessed according to these factors. Detailed plans to provide for consultancy, supervision, evaluation and training needs can then be drawn up on a team basis, and resource implications calculated. Some resources will be beyond the immediate influence and control of the team, but those teams which develop clear work objectives and coherent staff development plans to match, will be in a strong proactive position to influence training officers, management and agency policy.

# Bibliography

*Note*: The bibliography includes all the references made in the book. The ones which are asterisked (\*\*for British publications, \*for others) are a selection of books, chapters and articles, which between them offer the reader a basic literature on social work consultation and supervision.

Abels, P. (1970) 'On the Nature of Supervision: The Medium is the Group', *Child Welfare*, 49 (reprinted in Munson, 1979)
\*Abels, P. (1977) *The New Practice of Supervision and Staff Development: A Synergistic Approach*, Chicago Assoc. Press
\*\*Ainley, M. and Kingston, P. (1981) 'Live Supervision in a Probation Setting', *Social Work Education*, 1(1)
Barclay Report (1982) *Social Workers: Their Role and Tasks*, Bedford Square Press
Barker, R.L. and Briggs, T.L. (1968) *Differential Use of Social Work Manpower*, New York: Nat. Assoc. of Social Workers
Blake, R.R. and Mouton, J.S. (1976) *Consultation*, Addison-Wesley
Brandon, J. and Davies, M. (1979) 'The Limits of Competence in Social Work: The Assessment of Marginal Students in Social Work Education', *Brit. J. of Social Work*, 9(3)
\*\*Briscoe, C. (1977) 'The Consultant in Community Work' *in* C. Briscoe and D.N. Thomas (eds.) *Community Work: Learning and Supervision*, Allen & Unwin
Brown, A. (1977) 'Worker-Style in Social Work', *Social Work Today*, 8(29)
Brown, A. (1979) *Groupwork*, Heinemann Educational Books
Brown, A. (1981) 'You've Got to Accentuate the Positive', *Community Care*, 5.2.81
\*\*Caplan, G. (1970) *The Theory and Practice of Mental Health Consultation*, Tavistock
\*\*Carpenter, J. (1984) 'Working Together: Supervision, Consultancy and Co-Working' *in* A. Treacher and J. Carpenter (eds.) *Using Family Therapy*, Basil Blackwell
Chelune, G. et al. (1979) *Self-Disclosure*, Jossey-Bass
Curnock, K. (1975) *Student Units in Social Work Education*, CCETSW Paper 11
Curnock, K. and Prins, H. (1982) 'An Approach to Fieldwork Assessment', *BJSW*, 12(5)
Danbury, H. (1979) *Teaching Practical Social Work*, Bedford Square Press
\*\*Davies, H. (1977) *Student Group Supervision*, Family Service Units
Davies, M. (1979) 'Fieldwork Failures – a very Rare Breed', *Community Care*, 20.9.79, 27.9.79 and 4.10.79
Davis, J. and Walker, M. (1982) 'Another time, another placement', *Social Work Today*, 13(46), 10.8.82
\*\*Davis, L. (1982) *Residential Care: A Community Resource*, Heinemann Educational Books (Chap. 4.)
\*\*Donnellan, P. (1981) 'Supervision in Groupwork' *in* J. Martel (ed.) *Supervision and Team Support*, Bedford Square Press
\*\*Downes, C. and Hall, S. (1977) 'Consultation Within Social Work', *Social Work Today*, 8(17), 1.2.77
Dyer, W.G. (1977) *Team Building*, Addison-Wesley
Errington, J. and Feeny, M. (1981) 'A Training Model for Intermediate Treatment Group Leaders', The Hilltop Intermediate Treatment Training Project, Save the Children Fund
Fizdale, R. (1958) 'Peer Group Supervision', *Social Casework*, 39, Oct 1958, (reprinted in Munson, 1979)

Freire, P. (1970) *Pedagogy of the Oppressed*, Harmondsworth, Penguin
Galinsky, M.J. and Schopler, J.H. (1980) 'Structuring Co-Leadership in Social Work Training', *Social Work with Groups*, 3(4)
\* Gallessich, J. (1982) *The Profession and Practice of Consultation*, Jossey-Bass
Garland, J. and Kolodny, R. (1966) 'A Model for Stages in the Development of Social Groups' *in* S Bernstein (ed.) *Explorations in Groupwork*, Boston University
\* Getzel, G. and Salmon, R. (1982) 'Group Supervision: An Organisational Approach', Paper given at the *4th Symposium for the Advancement of Social Work with Groups*, Toronto
Gibran, K. (1923, 1975) *The Prophet*, New York: Knopf
Goldschmied, E. (1982) Personal Fellowship Report, University of Bristol, (unpublished)
Harlesden Community Project (1979) *Community Work and Caring for Children*, Ilkley, Yorkshire, Owen Wells
\*\* Hawkins, P. (1982) 'Mapping it Out', *Community Care*, 22.7.82
Hawthorne, L. (1979) 'Games Supervisors Play', *Social Work (US)*, 20, (reprinted in Munson, 1979)
Heron, A. (1978) *in* B. Proctor's *Counselling Shop*, Chap. 9, Burnett Books
Heron, A. (1975) *Six Category Intervention Analysis*, University of Surrey
Holder, D. and Wardle, M. (1981) *Teamwork and the Development of a Unitary Approach*, Routledge & Kegan Paul
Hollis, F. (1964) *Casework: A Psychosocial Therapy*, New York, Random House, p.272
Hughes, J. (1980) Personal Fellowship Report, University of Bristol (unpublished)
Insley, V. (1959) 'Social Work Consultation in Public Health' *in* G. Caplan (ed.) *Concepts of Mental Health and Consultation*, US Printing Office
Johnson, D.W. and Johnson, F.P. (1975) *Joining Together: Group Theory and Group Skills*, Prentice-Hall
Jones, M. (1976) *Maturation of the Therapeutic Community*, Human Science Press, NY
\* Kadushin, A. (1969) 'Games People Play in Supervision', *Social Work (US)*, 13 (reprinted in Munson, 1979)
Kadushin, A. (1974) 'Supervisor-Supervisee: A Survey', *Social Work (US)*, 19 (reprinted in Munson, 1979)
\* Kadushin, A. (1976) *Supervision in Social Work*, Columbia University Press
\* Kadushin, A. (1977) *Consultation in Social Work*, Columbia University Press
\* Kaslow, F. (ed.) (1977) *Supervision, Consultation and Staff Training in the Helping Professions*, Jossey-Bass
\*\* Kingston, P. and Smith, D. (1983) 'Preparation for Live Consultation and Live Supervision', *Journal of Family Therapy*, 5, 219–233
Lewis, J. and Gibson, F. (1977) 'The Teaching of Some Social Work Skills: Towards a Skills Laboratory', *Brit. J of Soc. Work*, 7(2)
Lippitt, R. and Lippitt, G. (1977) 'Consulting Process in Action' *in* J. Jones and J. Pfeiffer, *The 1977 Handbook for Group Facilitators*, Univ. Associates
Maple, F.F. (1977) *Shared Decision Making*, Sage Publications
\*\* Mattinson, J. (1975) *The Reflection Process in Casework Supervision*, Institute for Marital Studies
McIlvanney, H. (1979) 'Motivation', article in *The Observer*, 18.11.79
\* Miller, I. (1960) 'Distinctive Characteristics of Supervision in Group Work', *Social Work (US)*, 5(1)
Morrell, E. (1979) 'A Lesson in Assessment', *Community Care*, 1.11.79
Morrell, E. (1980) 'Student Assessment: Where are we now', *Brit. J. of Social Work*, 10(4)
\* Munson, C. (ed.) (1979) *Social Work Supervision*, The Free Press
North, C. (1982) 'A Working Agreement', *Community Care*, 5.8.82

Parsloe, P. (1981) *Social Services Area Teams*, Allen & Unwin
**Parsloe, P. and Hill, M. (1978) 'Supervision and Accountability' *in* O. Stevenson and P. Parsloe (eds.) *Social Services Teams: The Practitioner's View*, Chap. VIII, DHSS
Parsloe, P. and Stevenson, O. (1979) 'Social Work Training: The Struggle for Excellence', *Community Care*, 8.11.79
**Payne, C. and Scott, T. (1982) *Developing Supervision of Teams in Field and Residential Social Work*, NISW, Paper No. 12
Payne, M. (1980) 'A Self-Positioning Exercise in a Social Work Course', *Social Work Education Reporter*, **28**(2)
Payne, M. (1982) *Working in Teams*, Macmillan
**Pettes, D. (1979) *Staff and Student Supervision*, Allen & Unwin
Priestley, P. *et al.* (1978) *Social Skills and Personal Problem Solving*, Tavistock
Prior, M. (1982) 'Professional Supervision and Staff Development', Personal Fellowship Report, University of Bristol (unpublished)
Reid, W. and Epstein, L. (*eds.*) (1977) *Task-Centred Practice*, Columbia University Press
*Reynolds, B. (1975) *Learning and Teaching in the Practice of Social Work*, New York: Farrar & Rinehart
Rogers, C. (1969) *Freedom to Learn*, Columbus, Ohio: Chas. Merritt
Rowbottom, R. and Bromley, G. (1980) 'Advisers, Development Officers and Consultants in Social Services Departments' *in* D. Billis *et al.*, (eds.) *Organising Social Services Departments*, Heinemann Educational Books
Sales, E. and Navarre, E. (1970) *Individual and Group Supervision in Field Instruction. A Research Report*, University of Michigan
Satyamurti, C. (1981) *Occupational Survival*, Blackwell
Scherz, (1958) 'A Concept of Supervision based on Definitions of Job Responsibility', *Social Casework*, 39 (reprinted in Munson, 1979)
Schwartz, W. (1971) 'On the Use of Groups in Social Work Practice' *in* W. Schwartz and S.R. Zalba, *The Practice of Group Work*, Columbia University Press
Searles, H.F. (1955) 'The Informational Value of The Supervisor's Emotional Experience' *in Collected Papers on Schizophrenia and Related Subjects*, The Hogarth Press (1965)
*Shulman, L. (1982) *Skills of Supervision and Staff Management*, F.E. Peacock
**Smith, D. and Kingston, P. (1980) 'Live Supervision without a One-Way Screen', *Journal of Family Therapy*, **2**, 379-87
Smith, P. (1980) *Group Processes and Personal Change*, Harper and Row
Stevenson, O. and Parsloe, P. (1978) *Social Services Teams: The Practitioner's View*, DHSS
**Street, E. (1981) 'The Family Therapist and Staff Group Consultancy', *Journal of Family Therapy*, **3**, 187-99
**Syson, L. (1981) *Learning to Practise*, CCETSW Study 3
Truax, C.B. and Carkhuff, R. (1967) *Towards Effective Counselling and Psychotherapy*, Chicago: Aldine
Tuckman, B.W. (1965) 'Developmental Sequences in Small Groups', *Psychological Bulletin*, **63**(6)
*Watson, K. (1973) 'Differential Supervision', *Social Work (US)*, **18**(6), 80-88
Weekes, J. Osborne, M. and Holgate, E. (1977) 'Supervision: a case for sharing', *Family Service Unit Quarterly*, 13, June 1977
**Westheimer, I. (1977) *Practice of Supervision in Social Work*, Ward Lock Educational
**Whiffen, R. and Byng-Hall, J. (eds.) (1982) *Family Therapy Supervision*, Academic Press
**Wright, G. (1978) 'A Model of Supervision for Residential Staff', *Social Work Today*, **9**(45)
**Young, P. (1967) *The Student and Supervision in Social Work*, Routledge & Kegan Paul

# Index

Abels, P., 74
agency
   accountability, 7, 31, 41, 57, 75, 79
   context for consultancy, xi, xiii, 7–8, 17
   expectations of consultancy, 16, 19, 42
   and external consultants, 43
   and professional development, 91–6
   as source of consultancy, 9–11, 28, 52–3
   and students, 61–2, 64–5
   and team-consultancy, 81–90
Ainley, M., 15

Barclay Report, 21, 94
Barker, R.L. and Briggs, T.L., 93
Blake, R.R. and Mouton, J.S., 54
Brandon, J., 72
Briscoe, C., 8, 9, 51
Bristol, 60
Bromley, G., 10
Brown, A., xiii, 7, 24, 73, 78

Caplan, G., 2, 3
career-development stages, ix–xii, 6, 19, 20–21, 37
Carpenter, J., 35
CCETSW, 5, 21
Chelune, G., 45
child-guidance clinics, 64, 82, 83
clients, i, ix, x, 30–1, 35, 49, 50–1, 60, 64, 67, 68, 72, 79, 81, 91, 93, 94
co-counselling, 12
community work, 8–9, 26, 29, 51–2, 68
confidentiality, 30–1, 67, 68, 69, 70, 80
consultancy
   components, 2
   contracts, xiii, 29–32, 76, 87–8
   definitions, 2–3

   focus, 30, 50–1
   group approaches, 17, 34, 38, 74–90
   and methods of social work, 8–9
   mirroring effect, 46–7
   need for, 6–9, 16–17, 27–8
   pitfalls and dilemmas, 39, 48–9
   preparation, 27–9, 42–3, 75
   purpose, 30
   skills, 39, 43–7
   sources of, xi, 6, 9–12, 39
   style, 9, 16
   techniques, xii, 31, 47–8
   types of, 12–17, 34–7
consultancy and supervision, 1–17
   components, 2
   context of, 7–8
   definitions and distinctions, 1–5
   'dual' model, xii
   functions, 2
   group approaches, 74–81
   and methods of social work, 8–9
   models and types, xii–xiii, 12–17
   need for, 6–9, 16–17, 20–1, 37
   and professional development, 91–6
   and student experience, 57
consultant, 39–55
   contact stage, 40–1, 87
   contract stage, 29–32, 41–2, 87–8
   internal, 51–3
   and joint work, 14
   matching, 9
   outsider (external), 11–12, 51–2, 84–90
   as participant, 12–17
   peer, 12–13
   preparation, 42–3
   pitfalls and dilemmas, 48–9
   recording, 43
   relationship with supervisors, 41–2, 49, 52
   roles, xiii, 1, 12–17
   selection of, 9, 28–9, 32
   skills, x, 39, 43–9, 54–5

source of, 9–11
style, 9, 25, 70
techniques, 47–8
training, 54–5
consultee, 18–38
  agenda preparation, 32
  career stage, 18–19
  in consultancy session, 18, 32–4
  contract, 18, 29–32
  expectations, 19–20
  learning-style, 18, 22–4, 37
  preparation, 18, 27–9, 30, 32
  proactive approach, x, 11, 18, 32, 37, 78
  relationship with consultant, xiii, 1, 14, 28–39
  risk-taking, 33, 49
  role-taking, 33
  selecting a consultant, 28–9, 40–1
  self-disclosure, 26, 36, 60
  skills, 18, 28–35
  stance and needs, 18, 27–8
  style, 37–8
  work-style, 18, 22, 24–7, 37–8
co-working and consultancy, xi, 9, 10, 12, 32, 33, 35, 40, 50–1
CQSW, xiii, 56, 57
crisis consultancy, 28–9
CSS, 57
Curnock, K., 66, 72, 81

Danbury, H., 56, 64
Davies, M., 72, 80, 81
Davis, J. and Walker, M., 71
Davis, L., 7, 86
day-care, ix, 7, 15, 29, 64, 71
Donnellan, P., 9
Downes, C., 40
Dyer, W.G., 83, 85

Errington, J. and Feeny, M., 15
evaluation and review, xiii, 5, 16, 30, 40, 46, 50, 66, 67, 68, 80, 89, 91, 94, 96
external (outside) consultancy, 11–12, 39, 43, 51–2, 84–90, 92

family therapy, 8–9, 14, 15, 26, 29, 48, 51, 60, 68, 81, 85, 87, 88, 89

fieldwork placements, 66–7
Fizdale, R., 75
Freire, P., 18

Galinsky, M.J. and Schopler, J.H., 9, 50
Gallessich, J., 55
Getzel, G. and Salmon, R., 80
Gibran, K., 39
Goldschmied, E., 9, 15
group consultancy, xiii, 13, 74–90
  advantages, 79–80
  contract, 76
  disadvantages, 80
  a distinctive method, 81
  an example, 77–8
  group composition and size, 75
  leader skills, 78
  member skills, 78–9
  preparation for, 75
  stages of development, 76, 83
group supervision, xi, xiii, 10, 13, 35, 48, 74–80, 86
  *see also* group consultancy
groupwork, xiii, 3, 5, 8–9, 26, 29, 33, 50–1, 71, 75, 77–8, 79, 87, 89, 94

Harlesden Community Project, 83
Hawkins, P., 55
Hawthorne, L., 37, 54
Heron, A., 12, 55
Holder, D. and Wardle, M., 80
Hollis, F., 21
hospitals, 8, 43, 64, 71, 82, 86
Hughes, J., ix, 19

in-agency consultancy, 10–11, 17, 39, 51, 52–3
individuals, work with, 8, 15, 26
Insley, V., 3
in-team consultancy, 9–10, 17, 39
intermediate treatment, 15, 68

Johnson, D.W. and Johnson, F.P., 25
joint work consultancy, 13–17
Jones, M., 88

Kadushin, ix, xii, 1, 4, 5, 6, 19, 29, 36, 41, 44, 55
Kaslow, F., 39, 79
Kingston, P., 9, 14, 15, 35

learning-style, 22–4
Lewis, J. and Gibson, F., 72
Lippitt, R., and Lippitt, G., 55
'live' consultancy and supervision, 9, 14–15, 34–5, 41, 49, 68, 94

McIlvanney, H., 25
management and managers
  bureaucratic and professional, x, 7, 9
  consultancy for, 6, 51–2, 94–5
  consultancy proposals, 83, 87
  functions of, xi, 1–2
  promotion of, ix
  and staff-development, 96
  and staff needs, 19–20
  and student-placements, 56
  threat of non-supervisor consultancy, 52–3, 79
  *see also* supervisor, team-leader
Maple, F.F., 77
Mattinson, J., 8, 46
'midstream' consultancy, 28
Miller, I., 9
Morrell, E., 72
multi-professional settings, 7–8, 82, 86
multi-worker consultancy, 30
Munson, C., xii

non-participant consultancy, 12–13, 16–17, 31–2, 34, 39
North, C., 36

'observed' consultancy, 12, 16–17, 39

Parsloe, P., ix, xi, 10, 11, 19, 71, 72, 82, 93
participant consultancy, 12, 13–15, 17, 31, 34–5, 38, 39, 49–50, 67
Payne, C. and Scott, T., 82, 96
Payne, M., 58, 82

peer-consultancy
  peer-pairs, 10, 12–13, 17, 34, 38, 41, 53–4
  peer-groups, 13, 35, 38, 39, 75, 79, 81
periodic 'on-site' consultancy, 9, 15, 35, 49
Pettes, D., x, xii, 1, 56, 64
practice-teacher
  assessment of practice, 72–3
  (first) contact with student, 63
  contract for placement, 63–4, 68, 70
  in joint work, 33–4, 69
  preparation for student, 64–6
  relationship with student, 57, 60–2
  role in student-learning, 59
  self-preparation, 65–6
  sharing supervision, 70–1
  in student units, 65–6
  titles, 1, 56
  and training-course, 65
  and visible practice, 66–9
Priestley, P. (*et al.*), x, 24
Prior, M., 2
Probation Service, 21, 60, 61, 64, 71, 75, 85, 86, 95
professional development, x, xi, 6, 91–6

Reid, W., (and Epstein, L.), x
residential work, ix, 7, 15, 30, 47, 49, 64, 66, 68, 71, 75, 82, 85, 86, 87, 96
Reynolds, B., 23
Rogers, C., 18
role-play, xii, 31, 32, 47–8, 73, 79, 85
Rowbottom, R., 10

Sales, E. and Navarre, E., 80
Satyamurti, C., ix, 19
Scherz, F., 18
Schwartz, W., 45
sculpting, xii, 31, 79, 85, 89
Searles, H., 46
self-positioning, 24, 58

# Index

Shulman, L., xii, 45, 54, 55, 78, 79
Smith, D., 9, 14, 15, 35
Smith, P., 45
Social Services Departments, ix, 11, 40, 71, 82, 85, 86
social skills, x, 68
social workers' needs, ix–xii
staff development, xiii, 6, 91–6
staff group consultancy, xiii, 6, 81–90
 see also team consultancy
Stevenson, O., ix, 10, 11, 71, 72
Street, E., 87
student (and student-placement)
 assessment, 72–3
 as consultant, 3
 games-playing, 61
 and group approaches, 81
 joint work with practice-teacher, 69
 learning skills, 59–60
 learning styles, xi, 22–4
 linked placements, 71
 placement aims, 57
 placement context, 57–8
 placement contract, 63–4, 68, 70
 placement preparation, 66
 preparation for supervision, 66
 self-management skills, 59, 60–2, 73
 stage, xiii, 1, 56–73
 stress-management, 62
 supervision,
  see student supervision
 tapes, use of, 69–70
 theory, application of, 71–2
 visible practice, xiii, 66–9
 work-style, 24–7, 60–2
student supervision
 agenda, 57–8
 assessment of practice, 72–3
 context, 57–8
 contract, 63–4
 when co-workers, 33–4
 importance of, xi, 20–1, 35, 56–7
 preparation for, 64–6
 shared, 70–1
 tapes, use of, 69–70
 theory, 58, 71–2

visible practice, 66–9
student units, 65–6, 81
supervisee
 evaluation of, 94
 expectations of supervision, 19–20
 games-playing, 36–7
 needs of, x
 relationship with supervisor, 1, 4, 21, 31, 35–7, 84
 see also consultee
supervision
 and consultancy, 1–17
 consultative, 2, 28–9, 37, 54–5
 contract making, 29–32, 35–36
 definitions and functions, 1–2
 distinctive features, 4
 games-playing, xiii, 36–7, 45
 educational, 2
 in groups, see group supervision
 managerial, 1–2
 need for, 6–9, 20–1
 professional, 2
 relationship, 1, 4, 19–21, 31, 35–7, 84
 skills of, 45
 student stage, xi, 56–73
supervisor
 confidentiality, 31
 as consultant, 28–9, 39
 contract-making, 35–6
 games-playing, 36–7, 45
 relationship with consultant, 41, 49, 52–3
 relationship with supervisee, 4, 19–21, 35–37, 84
 role, x, 1
 role-model, xi, 56
 skills, 45, 49, 54–5
 and team-consultancy, 81–90
Syson, L., 56, 62, 67, 71

tandem consultancy, 12–13, 17
tape-recordings, xii, 16, 48, 55, 68, 69–70
task-centred casework, x
team(s)
 characteristics of, 82–3, 92
 collective, xi, 82, 91

composition, 88, 91–2, 96
culture, 95–6
definitions, 82
individualistic, xi, 82
meetings, 85
objectives, 92, 96
and professional development, 91–6
resources, 92–3
sibling rivalry in, 36
and social work practice, 67
source of consultancy, 9–10
and students, 64–5, 70
supervision, *see* group supervision
team consultancy, 81–90
away-days, 85, 92
motivation, 83–4
need for, 29, 83
self-help models, 10, 85
skills, 86–90
stages, 89–90
tandem-teams, 85
team-leaders, ix, xi, 2, 9–10, 21, 64, 81, 84–5, 88, 93–6
training
and consultancy needs, ix–xi
for consultants, 54–5

definition of, 5–6, 81
in-service, xiii, 5
post-qualification, xiii, 5, 21, 93
and professional development, 37, 91–6
student-stage, 20, 56–73
techniques, 48, 55, 68
Truax, C.B. (and Carkhuff, R.), 44
Tuckman, B.W., 76, 83
tutor
integration of learning, 72
preparation for placement, 66
role in student-learning, 56, 59
in three-way contract, 63
'tutorial' consultancy, 12, 34

video, xii, 16, 31, 32, 48
visible practice, xiii, 7, 66–9

Watson, K., 12
Weekes, J., 14
Westheimer, I., x, xii, 2, 24
Whiffen, R. (and Byng-Hall, J.) 8, 14
work-style, 24–7
Wright, G., 7

Young, P., 56, 64

*Acknowledgement*
Many thanks to Gina Coleman for typing this index.